High Shelf

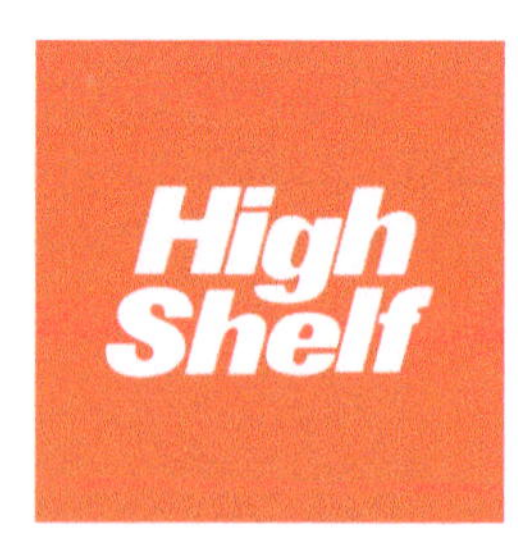

High Shelf Issue XVIII. May 2020.
Portland, Oregon.
Copyright 2020, High Shelf Press

ISBN: 978-1-7342842-9-4

Cover Image by Bill Schulz
Design, Layout and Editing by C. M. Tollefson
With special thanks to David Seung & River E. Hall

High Shelf Press reserves all rights to the material contained herein for the contributors protection; upon publication, all rights revert to the artists.

High Shelf XVIII

May 2020

"... i swallow a queen bee before i approach the altar and tell myself next week
will be different
i pull my collar higher to cover the
thorns, apple-red bites growing out of my neck
The Priest cries power into gold filigree and performs a miracle
the bell rings to tell us something has happened here..."

Matthew Bettencourt

“...hell forever
reinevents itself...”

Naomi Rhema Edwards

Table Of Contents

Prey Space in Geographies

Grace Sutphin

A boy hits an orange open with his baseball bat
and the pieces fly through prey space

A bird could, in perfect imitation,   fall
worldly and practical into the distance out

Where the land takes bodies that it cannot
keep, that it will leave dead and unexplored

in the small reach of shallow water
where heat is trapped and cooled

The wide river of   the innermost
The wide river of   the uncountable

Private hells re-conceived under the
promise of purpose, the propriety of   being

I left my fingers in the door of the
prey space bathroom and felt it close

I want to be told that I am subtle
in prey space, with my own limbs at a   minimum

The ferocious want for nothing is
the full knowledge of desire, look at what

can be afforded in prey space. Look at
what I have made available only   here

The bodies on the shore, the parts never again
whole, the flesh of your own ruminant animal.

Occasional Visit

Jason Hackett

The glow under the bedroom door
flickers blue

from the muted TV.

I sketch in the spackled ceiling,
fill in faces with seconds

& I wait for Old Smoke to return.

His urn is buried
on the top shelf of our closet

because "underground is too permanent."

He often sneaks out
for a chat after his daughter's

sleeping pills kick in

& I greet him with a stale cigarette
he bought tax-free on the reservation.

He has cut back from three packs

and has never felt better
in all his life, he winks.

He asks how it tastes,
how his grandchildren are doing,

if we've yet sold his place,

I blow four rings his way
& watch them break upon his face;

a kiss, I say, from each

family member. Before he goes,
I ask him to take his pack and

put it back in its hiding spot,

his urn. Shove it way down
into his gray bones and skin,

down deep,

into the dark place
his daughter never dares to dig.

Self Portraits

Robert Oehl

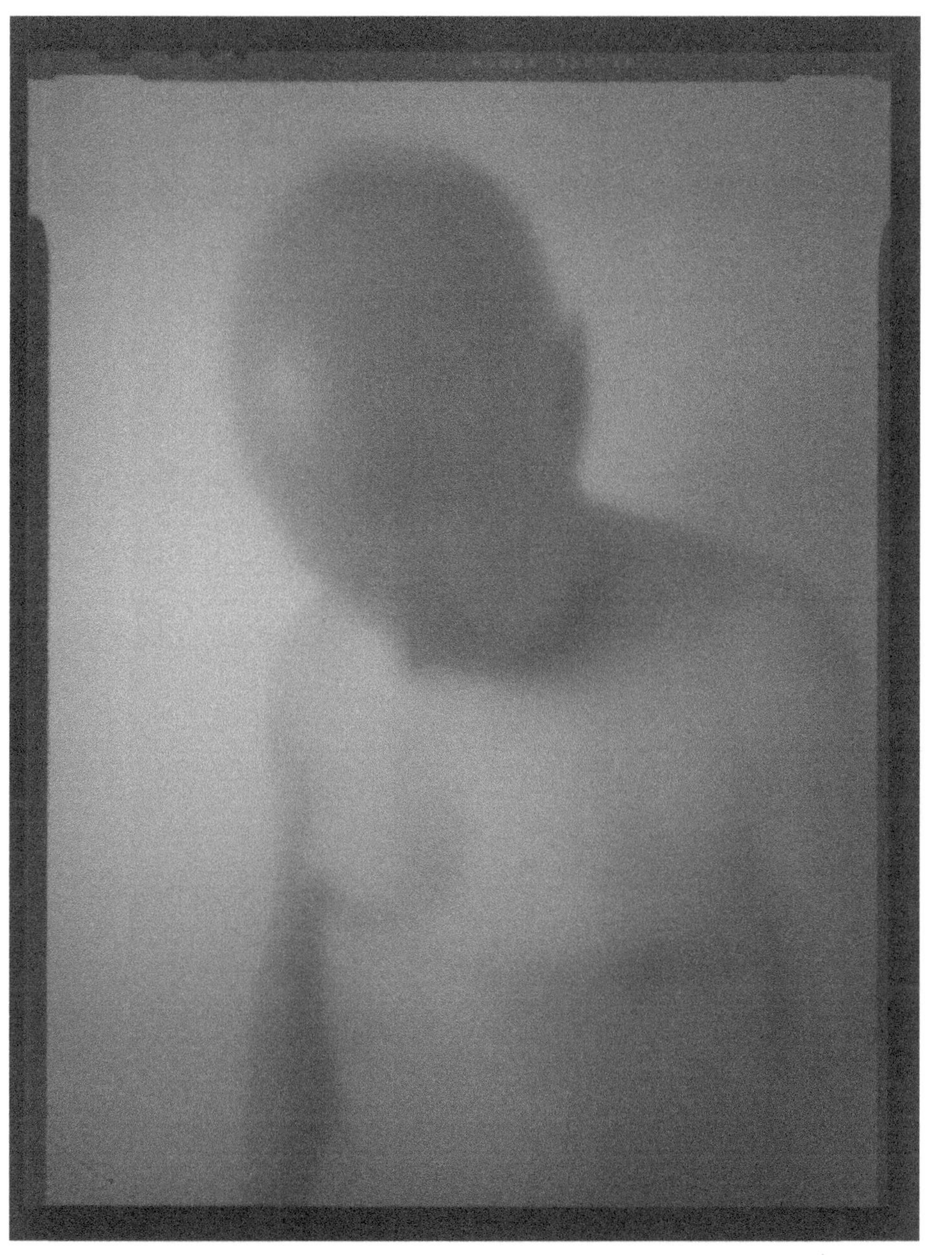

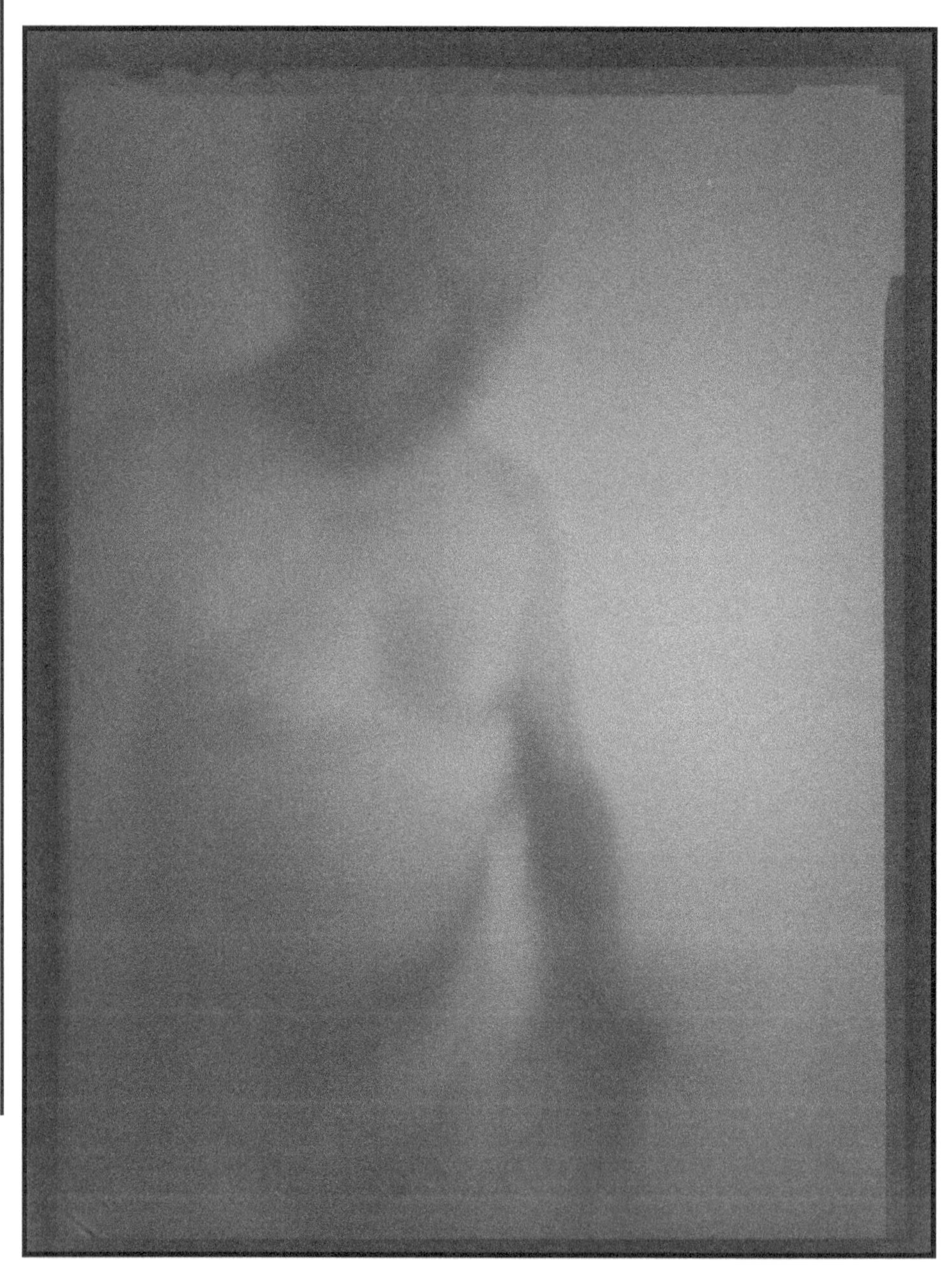

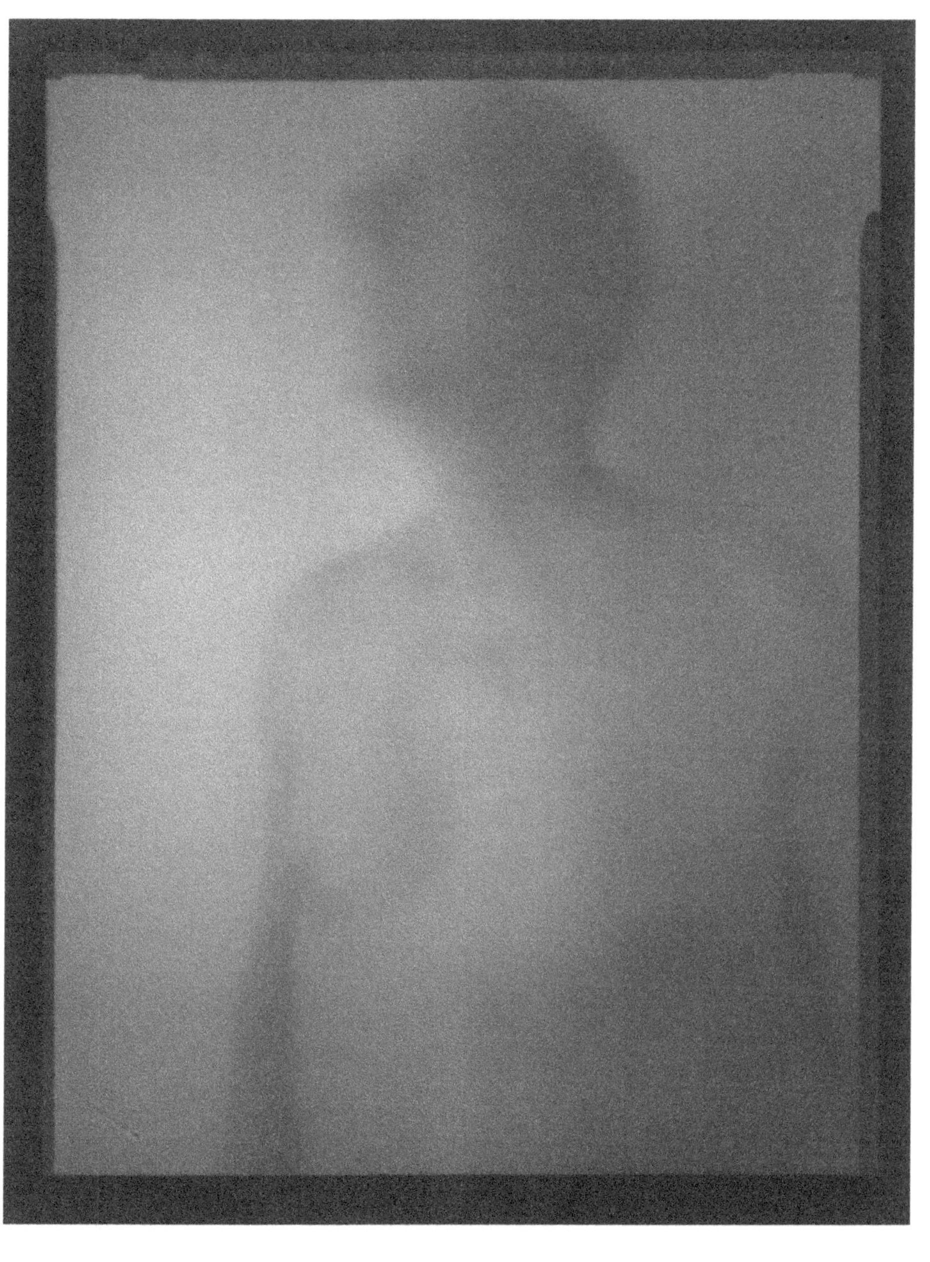

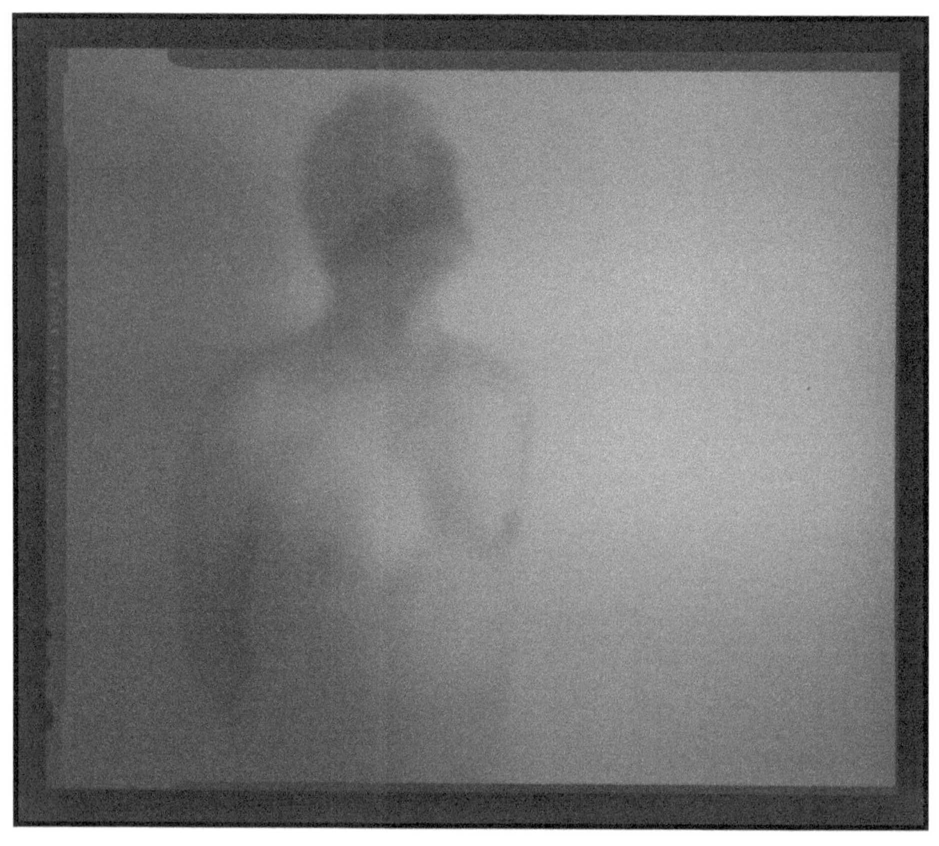

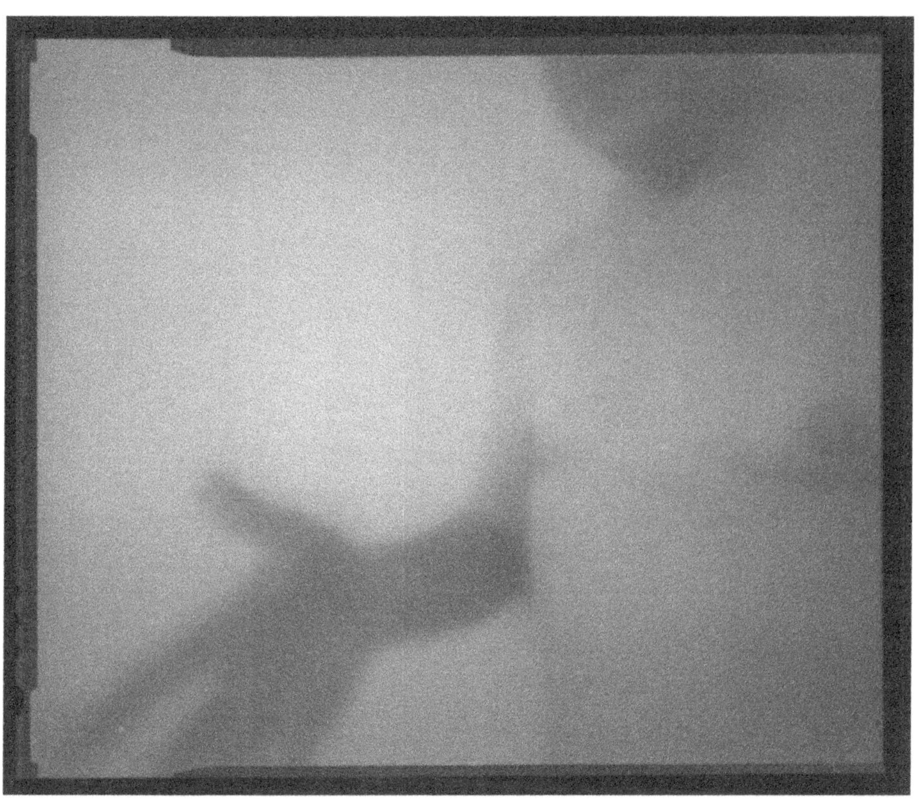

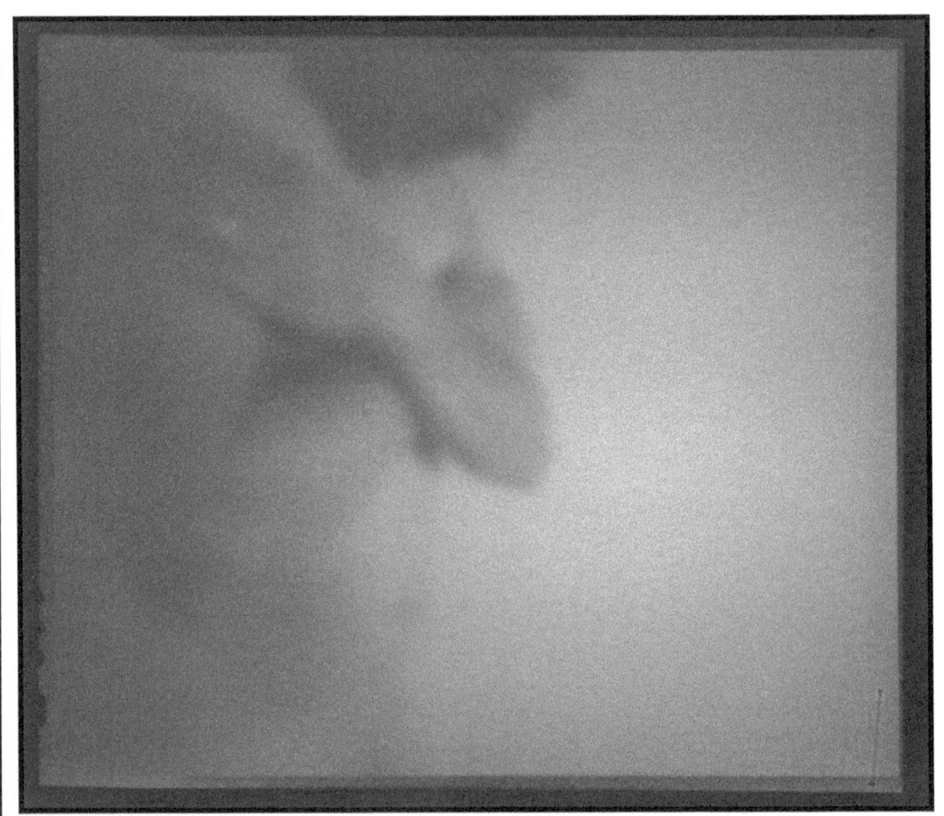

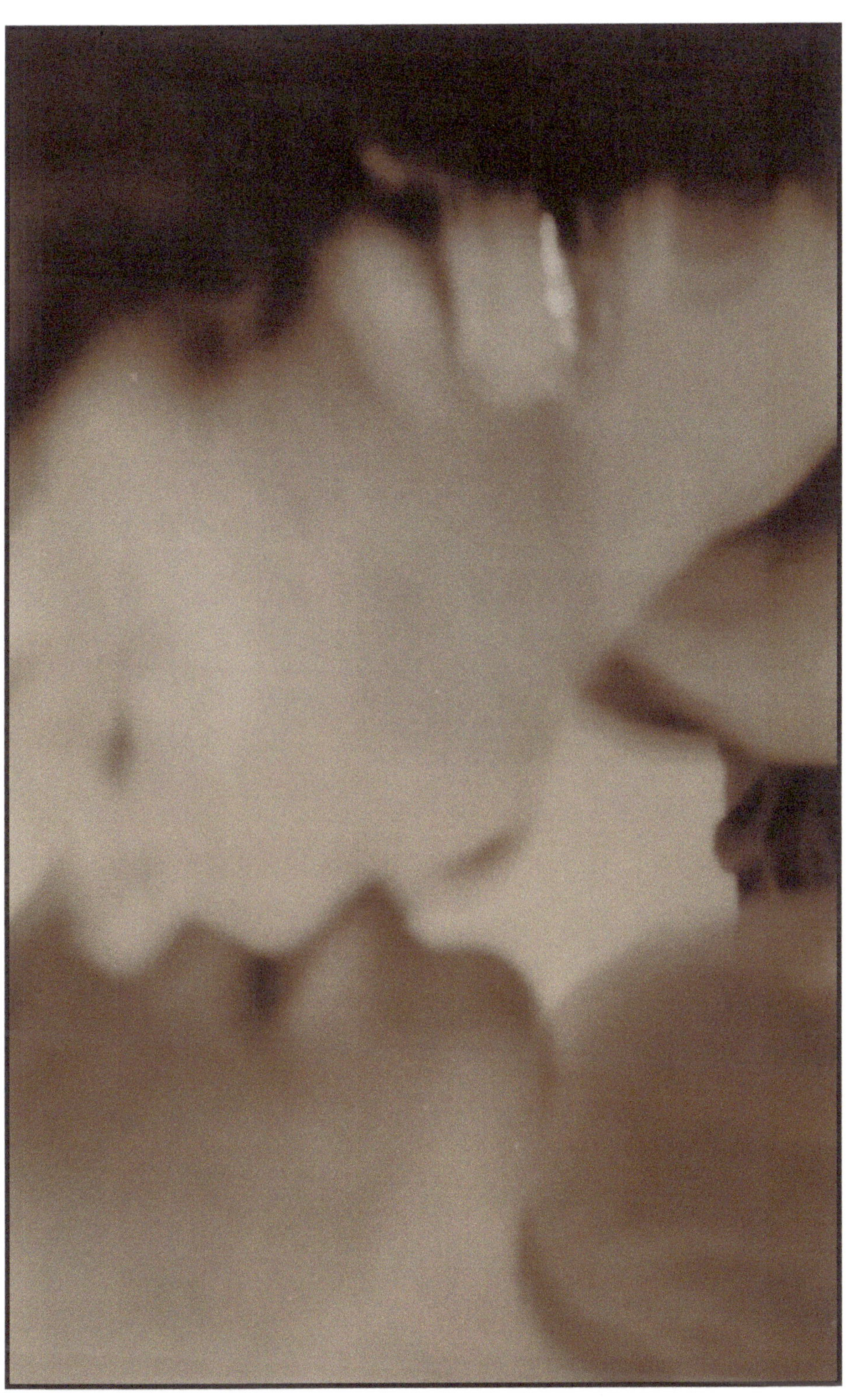

Church Bells

Matthew Bettencourt

we glowed sallow in
shatter-flicker fluorescent light, shine like
glass in those dim worm tunnels,
sweat-sticky skin in windowless corner rooms, the flood
waits for the door to shut before He walks the linoleum mile
back to his office nailed to the wall but we know
His ear slips between the cracks in our faith
anyways

Jane Brooks, Witch, was hung in 1658 because
she gave a boy an apple, touched his Right Side,
and lifted him over a garden wall.
Jane Brooks, Witch, is dead, but when we sneak
into the courtyard, red brick climbing to heaven on
four sides,
i wonder if she isn't strong enough to scale even those, if
she promised the boy Power when all he knew was
marble every thursday, lungs full of the sickly-sweet smoke
prayers rising
and He floated on His own

i swallow a queen bee before i approach the altar and tell myself next week
will be different
i pull my collar higher to cover the
thorns, apple-red bites growing out of my neck
The Priest cries power into gold filigree and performs a miracle
the bell rings to tell us something has happened here

I crack a bead of amber under my palm and breathe through gritted teeth
the shards stick in My hand, pass beneath the skin, and melt onto bone
I slice my thumb on bloodstone and it tells me a tornado is coming
this, I imagine, is what an apple tastes like when it's presented but not offered
over the walls, wind begins to whirl. a bell chimes
I wait

Wrong River

Naomi Rhema Edwards

Where there is salt there is
water, where there is salt there are scattered
the echoes of stars.

Star fields, sliding along
the walls of the mind

long

after the projectionist
is hanged   still I see him swinging in my empty mind

casting loops of shadow, becoming
clockwork.

Absorbed into the big
big big
machine keeps time.

      The most terrible concept of all, God agreed. *The awful project. And yet I said it, so it will be so. Let there be time, let it be kept, may its territory be so bound.*

      Meanwhile, how relentlessly my friends have died! Three in one winter, now again another, come the summer, still another, gone

oh well fell down a

      Here I'm dancing in a club again
broken glass in Berlin
cigarette tumbling down my shirt
              a shooting star, I vomit, joyous

someone drags me out of bed by the foot

Dublin, 2007   it's a case of mistaken identity   *sorry, sweetheart*
thought you were someone else

so did I

        drank too much and fell   in the incorrect river

       the one whose currents
       I don't know

that was a case of mistaken identity   sure

       but now let us think of those rivers, *right* rivers
       whose black-green nightly depths
       tumulted me

       sober, sober, set me right, set me   cold and wide awake
       tumbling over under water treefall to the
       railroad tracks

where Jon was waiting, drunk
on Southern Comfort, with the knife   to make us brothers

though I'm just a stupid girl, I
can be a brother to the one
whose death   too stupid to foretell, I was just

dancing by a river
clogged with ghosts   before its oily water

caught on fire
before I saw the heron with its wings of flame

       hell forever
       reinvents itself

stop the reel
    for a suicide break.

Or maybe we are not
yet death, oh Jonathon, maybe   I thought   *this is as bad as it gets*

       wrong river, wrong city   *wrong needle wrong knife*

but now I know there is no 'as it gets'
oh it gets
bad bad bad   it sure gets

bad   *I'm sorry, I do, I do*   *I do believe in suicide*

       in irrevocable invitations

come, let's be
brothers

     our humiliation enjoyed pre-emptively, then gotten over, yes? The projectionist agrees, his feet
     enact agreement

oh why why a river when I wanted the sea
give me salt that shrivels me to the size I really am
in homage to the God who understands me   who decreed there is no bottom, it just keeps
going down
down down

(and it is said, and it is good)

like the quarry where the boy who drowned his dog was drowned by other boys, who also drowned,
and the townies and the schoolkids fistfight broken bottle broken glass red busted taillight cadillac, red
rose red wine big dance bare ass yes yes I saw that movie too where is the beautiful girl losing her grip
on the wheel

(stop the reel)

who's the quarry now, yeah

     answer the question, who

now

               Shall we gather at the
               beautiful that beautiful that

river

               where the heron burned to black tangles of wire
               where my drunken guts have myriad myriad
               spewed

Yes, gather, ye
saints

we are to be ignited with the spirit   baptized   lest we be too old   to suicide.

                 As a child I came up
                 from the river's silty heart thrust
                 into daylight   crowning

in a cloud of biting flies

spitting and choking, wishing
I came from the sea

give me that cold clear Aeagean   or, come on
give me something

so I can say   *those hulking monsters in the water are just
islands, wait for the sunrise, then you'll
understand*

The Grainy In-Between

John Sexton

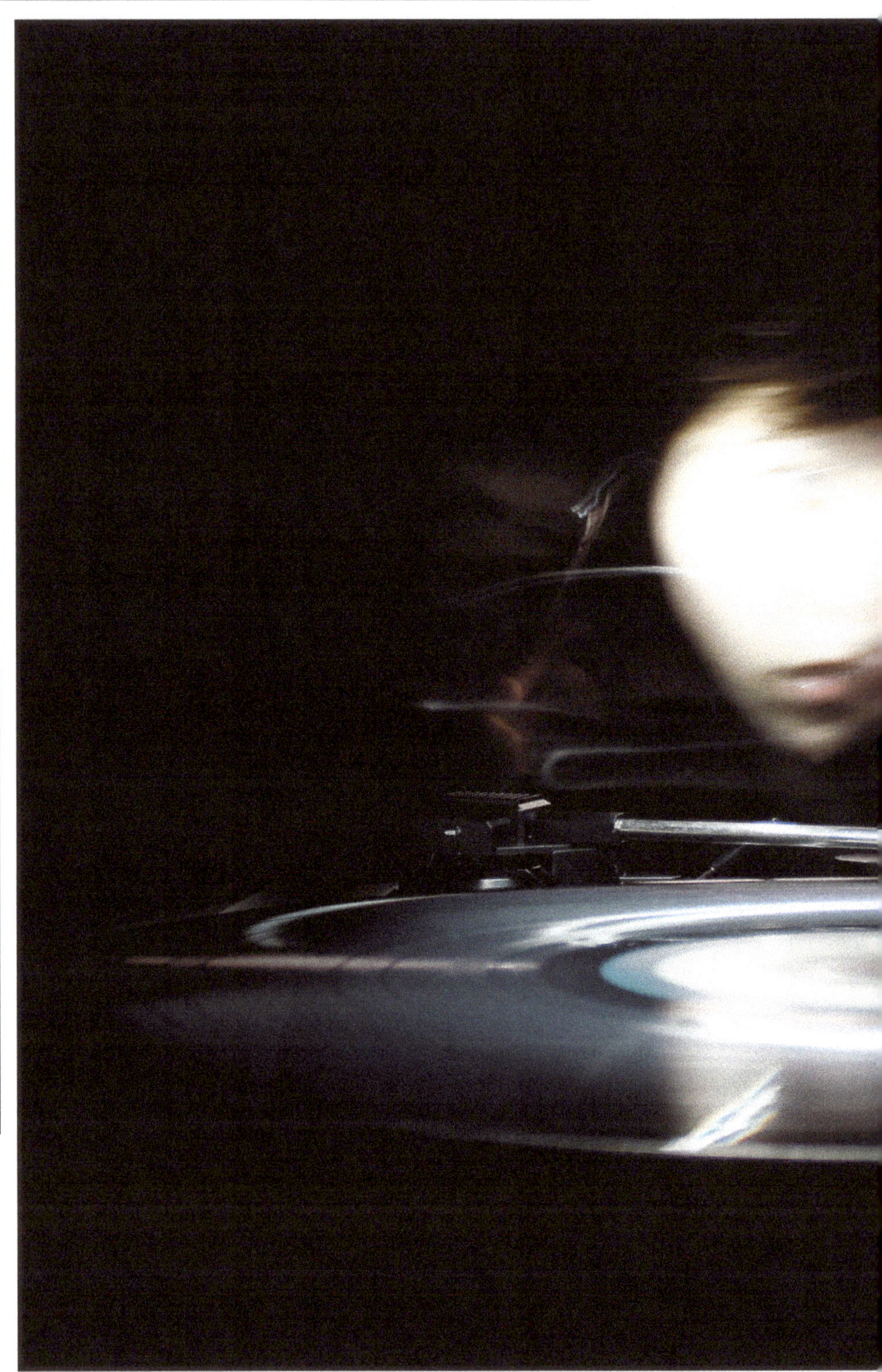

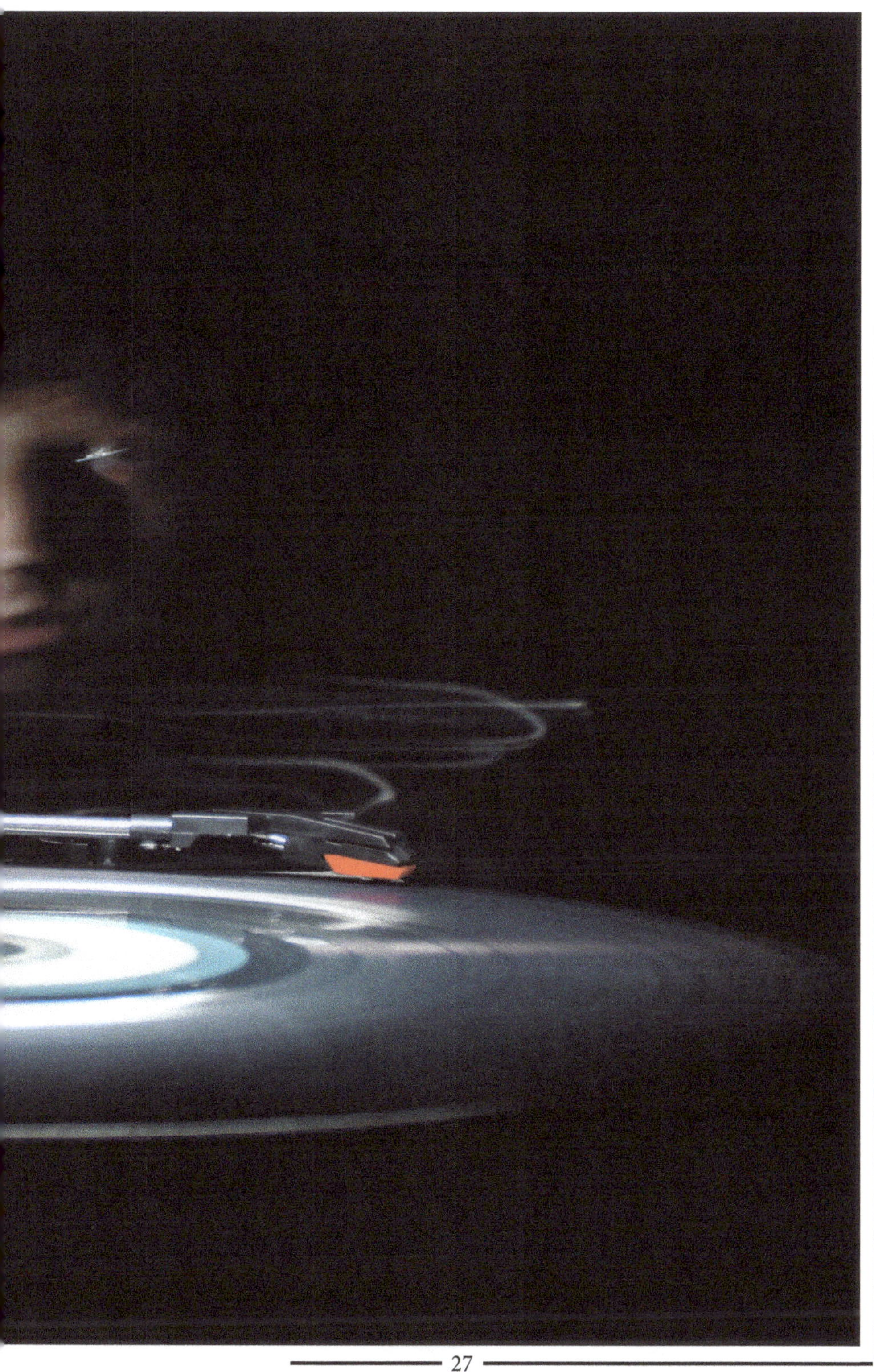

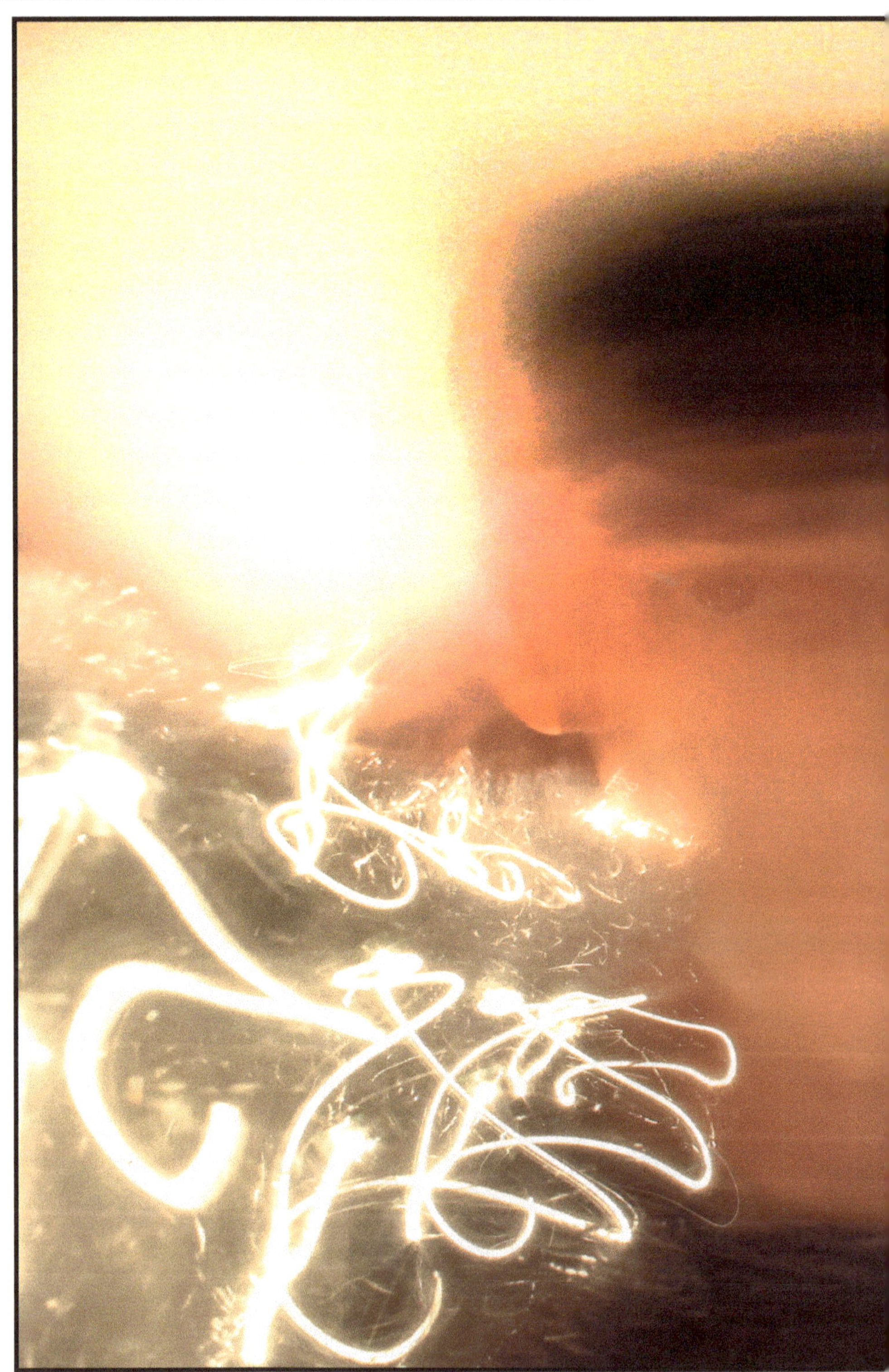

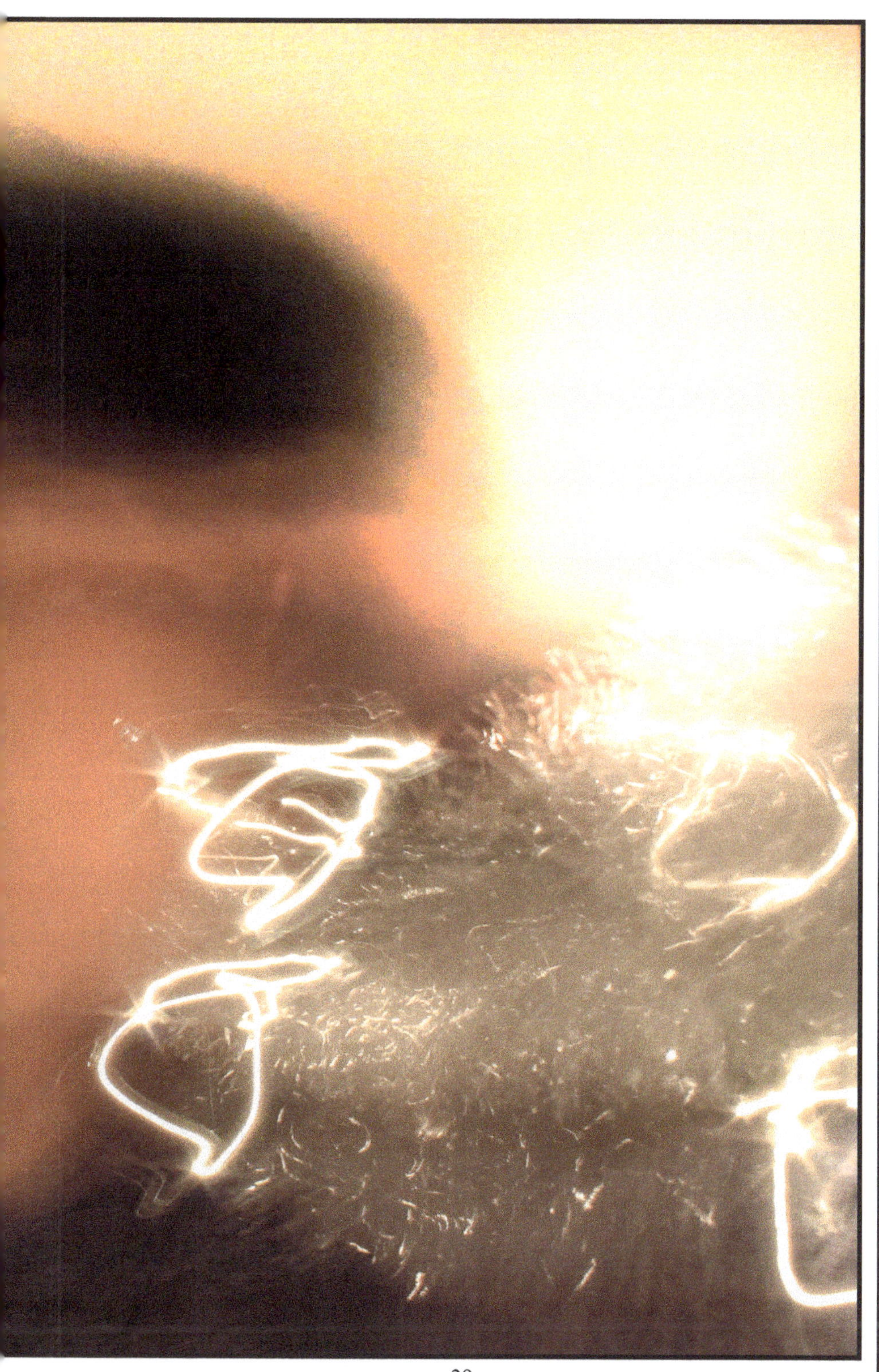

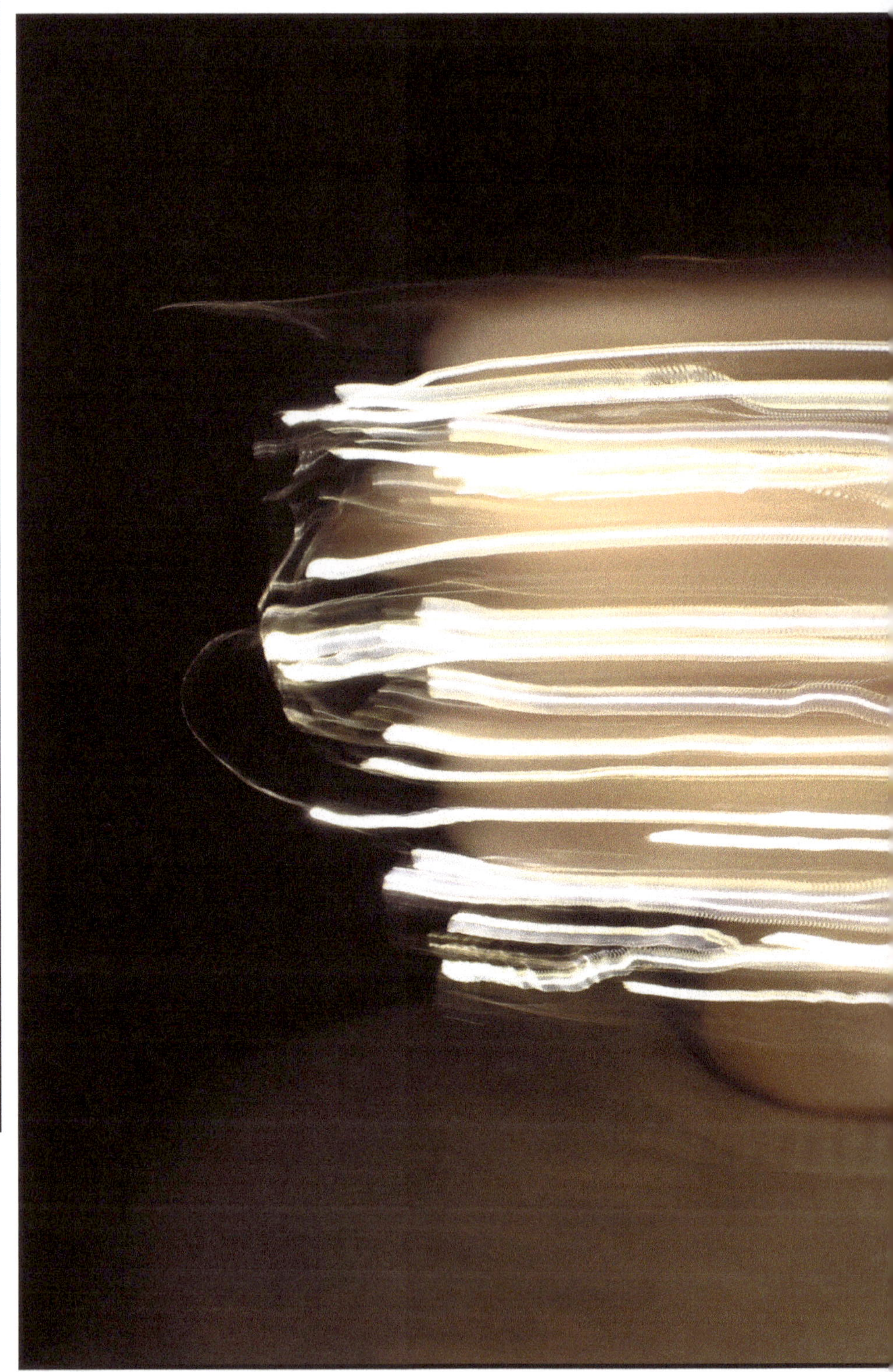

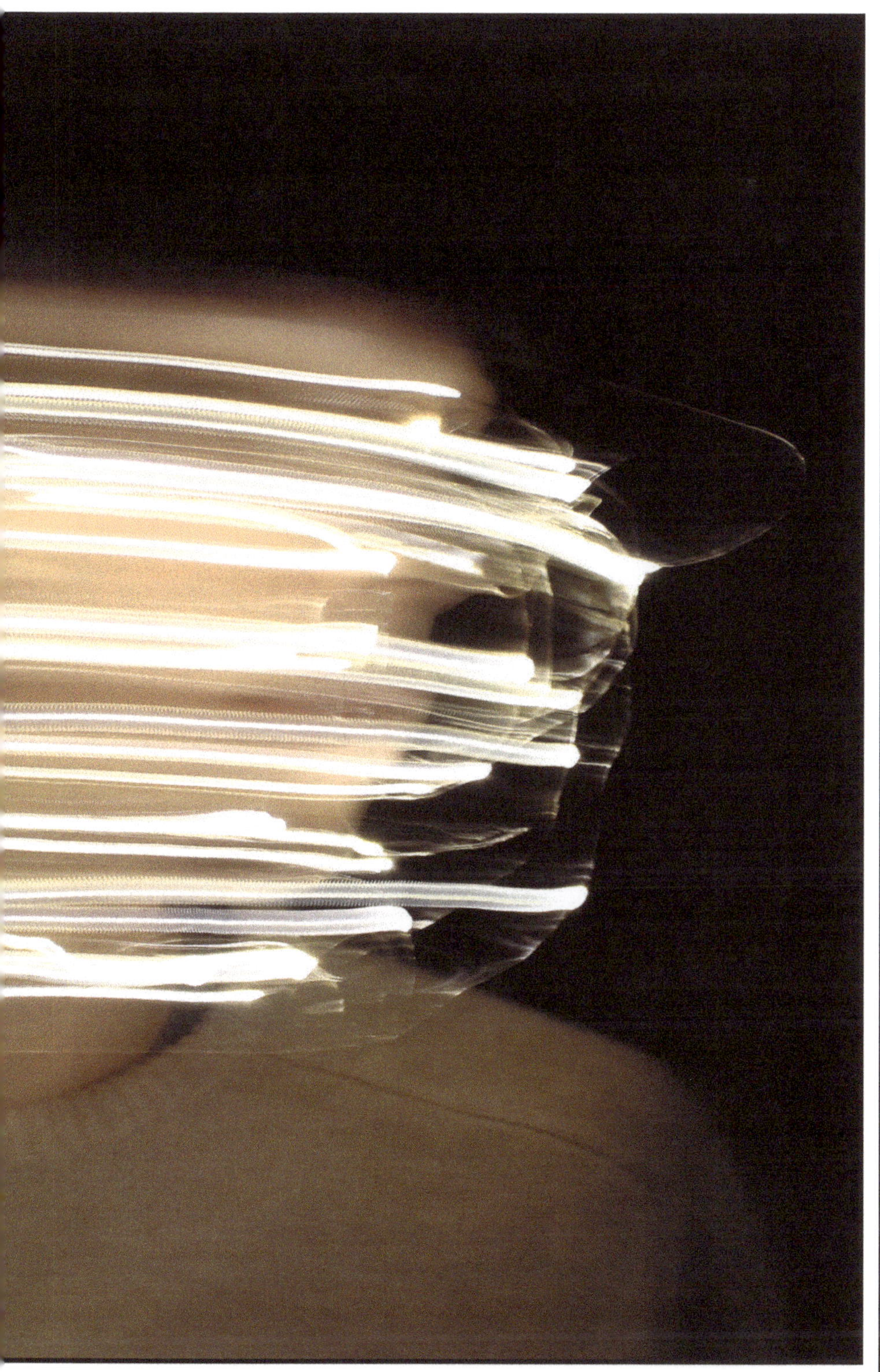

Buck-Shot Yellow Jackets

Skylar Rush

My lost things, these two.
What you wish to be listening to,
it finds you and darkens the darkness.
Skeletal tulip tree branches, enriching a soundscape
more cruel by far than thunder—the warning you doubt,
though you cannot afford the doubt. They remember. I know they do.
The dark monstering, the dark deviling, the whispering in-
breath echo of subvocal expression. The soaked things
shivered. I took their heads in my hands and
their eyes had brightened with fear-joy. The
one asked, "Will there be some music?"
The other said, "You could hear
how cold it was." Dampening
my chest, it reaches you
through the
chambers
you have
abandoned.
"Have you
heard?"
asked
the
one.
Then came the quiet.
"Three," said the one, stirred.
"Two," said the other, burbling.
There was a sucking-through-teeth sound, the
sounds that did not take the shape of words. Reverberating
tickatickas, cuck-cuck calls, bowel-guttering stridulations, sonic markers
of any kind. Ultrasonic, too high to be audible. The scornful echoes. Slapped.
"And of what temperature were the sounds?" I asked as I
evaluated what I collected; what I collected is poetry
that degenerated to science under my successful
scrutiny and reverted to song under my failing
love. The commentary stung like
buck-shot yellow jackets, like
adults betraying children,
the screams, the moans,
the creaks, the bone-
scraping vertigo-
inducing thumps.
No music? No
creation of
timbre? Of
lifts and
breaks in
voice?
It will
be a
long
night.

Bitter Lemon, Butter and Eggs

Caitlin Dunn

I think I know now

not all yellow flowers are

buttercups, not all

black birds are blackbirds

it's such a rare gift to see

clearly—to look for

the whiskers on cat

birds, not break even and call

them *mimidae*—most

of us give up when

we pry the binomen out

of them—my mother

says you can't *just* look

the difference between toad

flax and snapdragons

is in the close breath

The Drowned Man

Gabrielle Tribou

We lost each other
under the fluorescent night
of warehouse rafters,
faces hidden by mouthless masks,
eyes fast with fear,

and made homes of walls and corners,
avoided the slouching hallways
of concrete sand dunes
and beat-worn trailer parks,
prepared to wait out
the choreographed nightmare
we had paid to see,
the calculated spectacle
of human sprawl and immensity,
£30 tax-free.

And afterwards, Burger King,
to share what little we had gleaned:
rusted scissors in a pond,
the well-lit moon folding like music
behind a streak-eyed birthday clown,
all the champagne gone.

And though we never
traced our names in the oil
of a mechanic's back
or climbed the metal stairs to Hollywood,
we did keep our masks,
and wear them, arriving home,
when we knocked on
our own apartment doors.

as seen

George L Stein

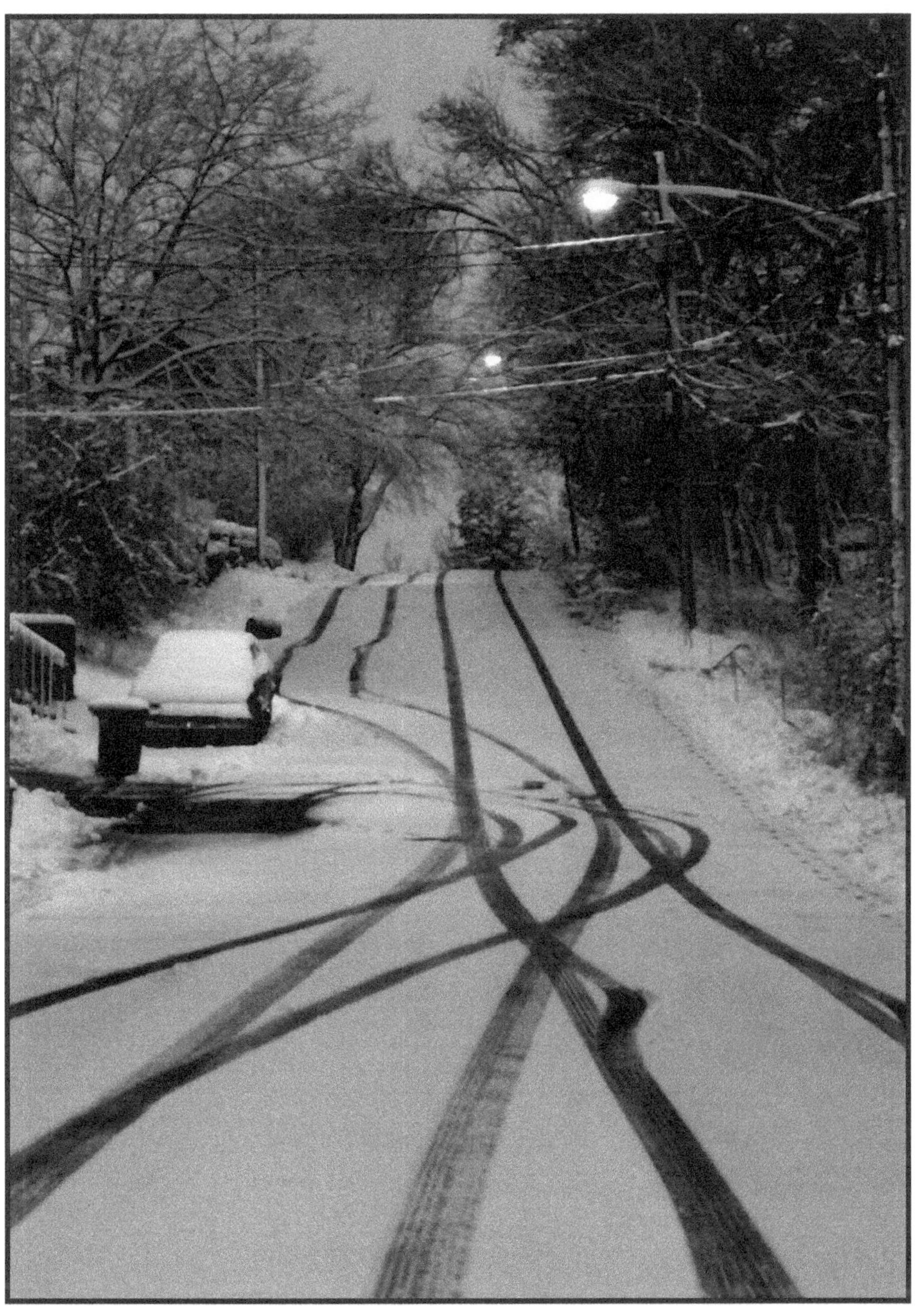

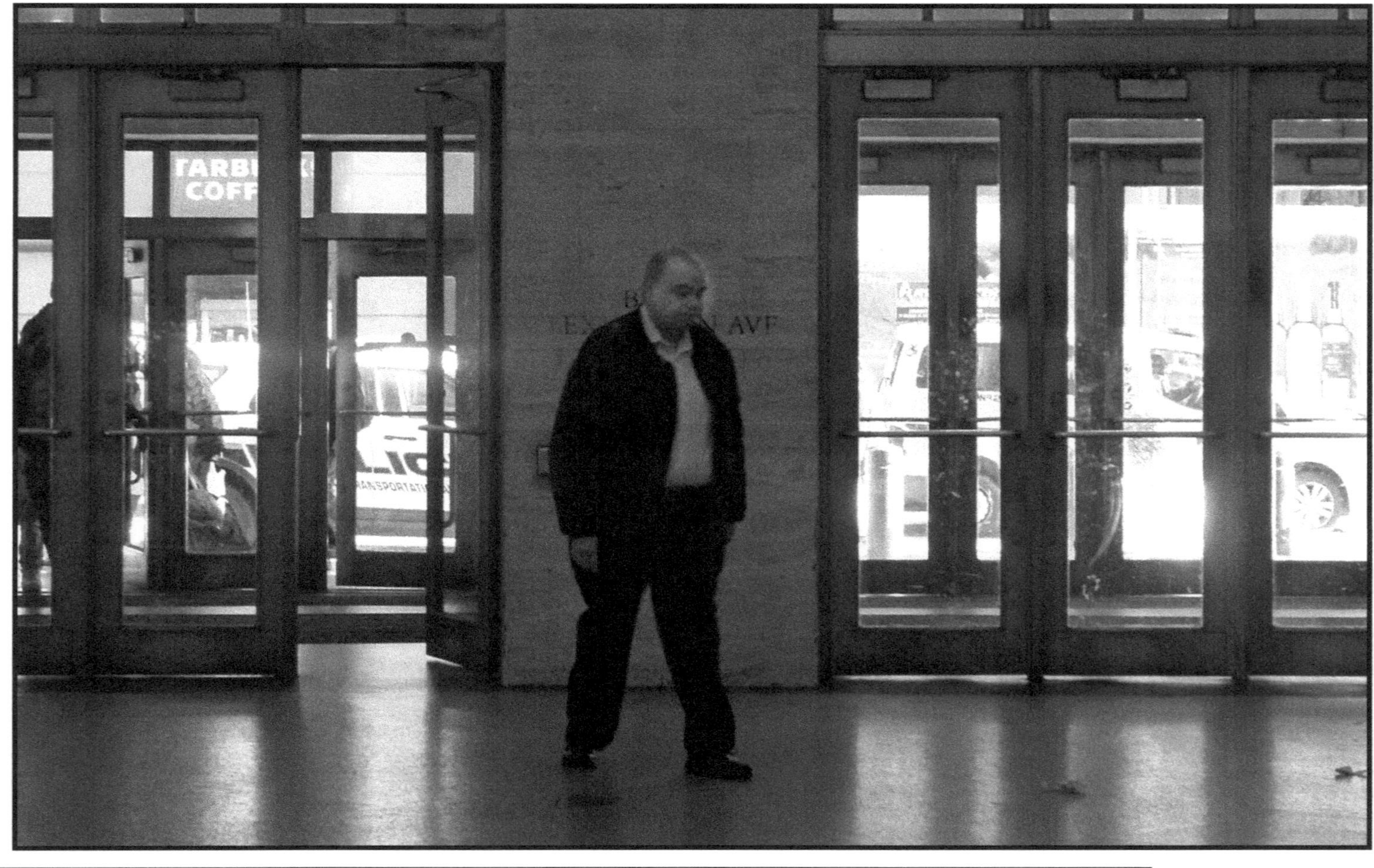
TARBUCKS
COFFEE

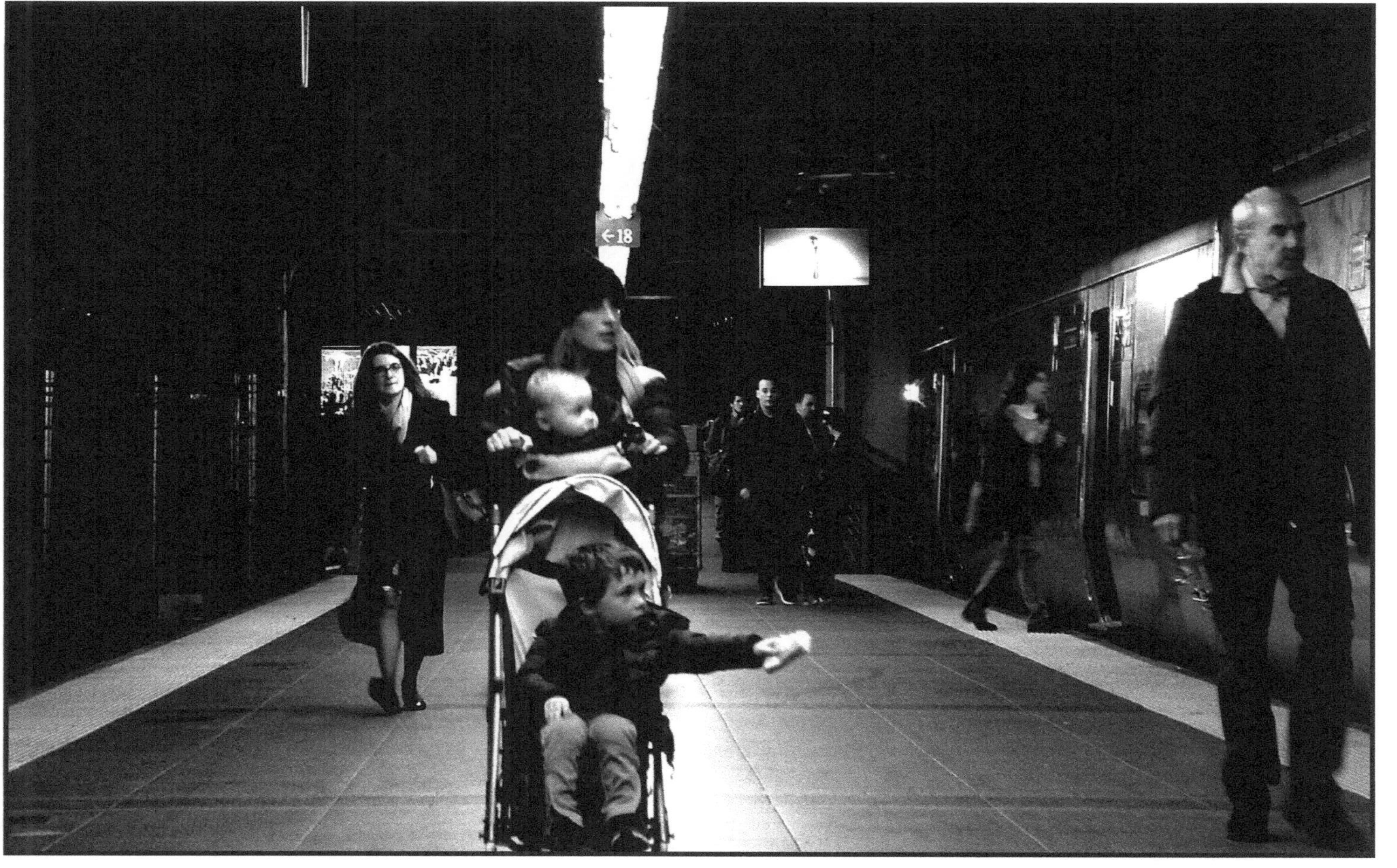
←18

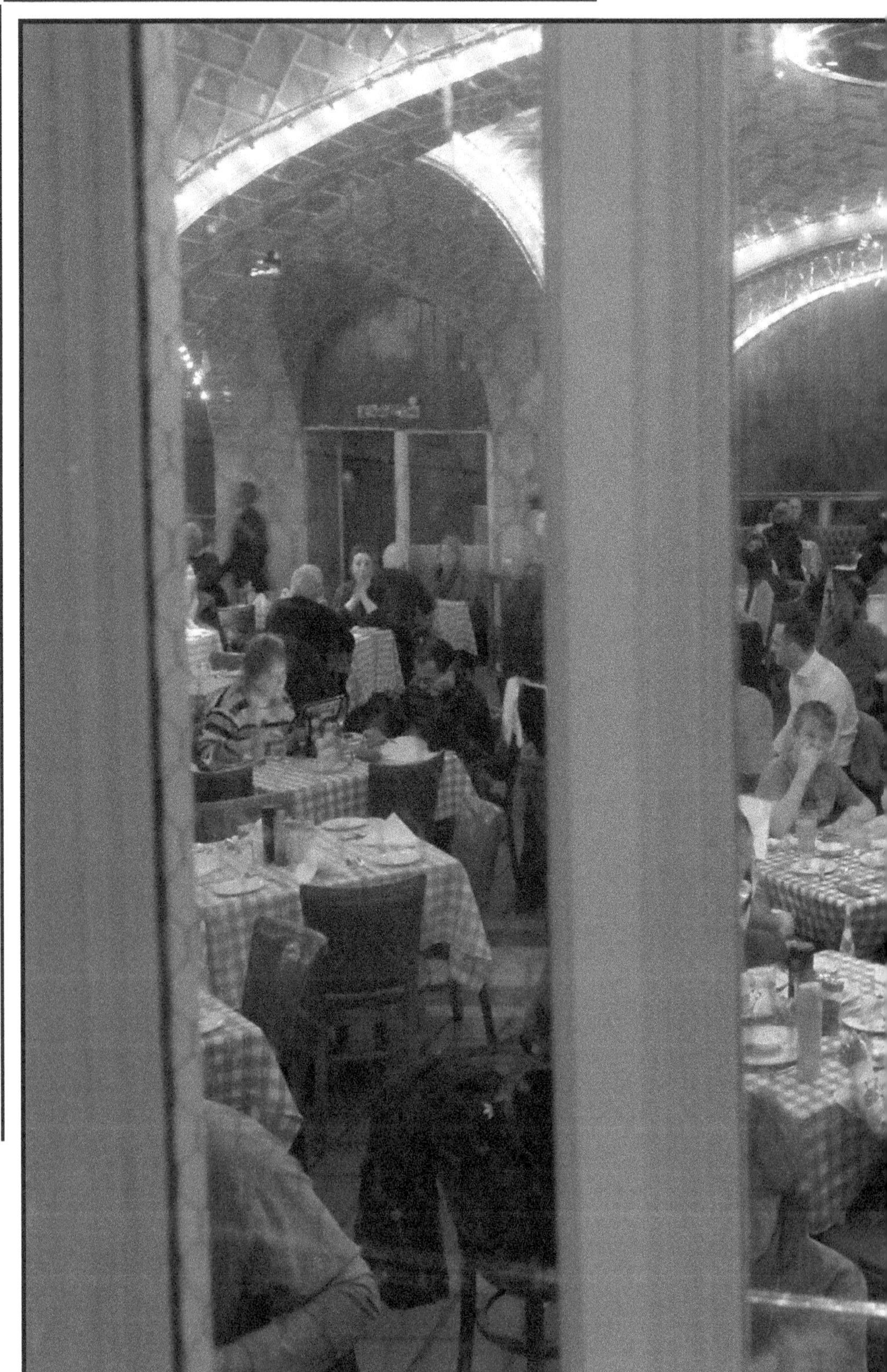

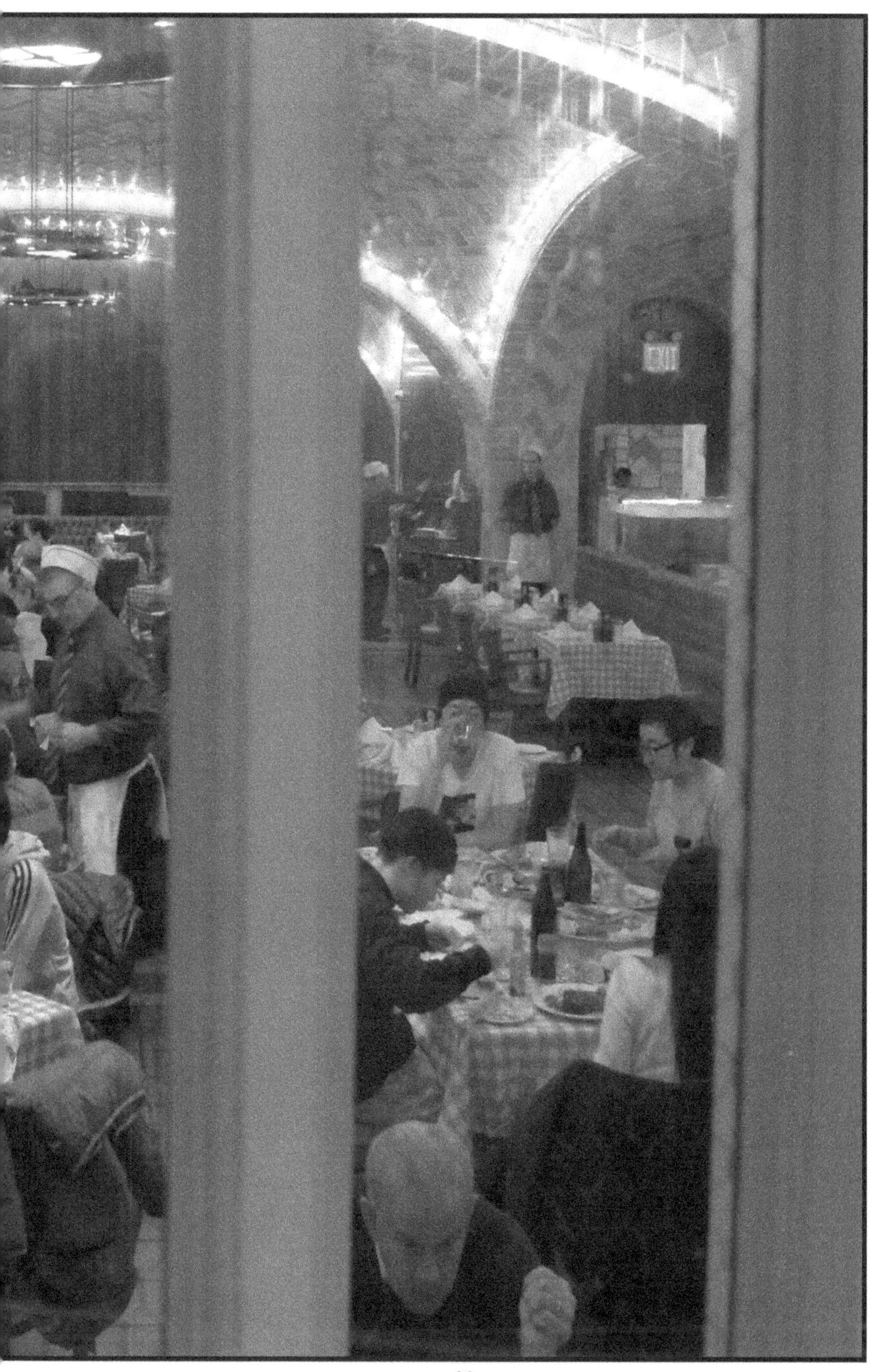

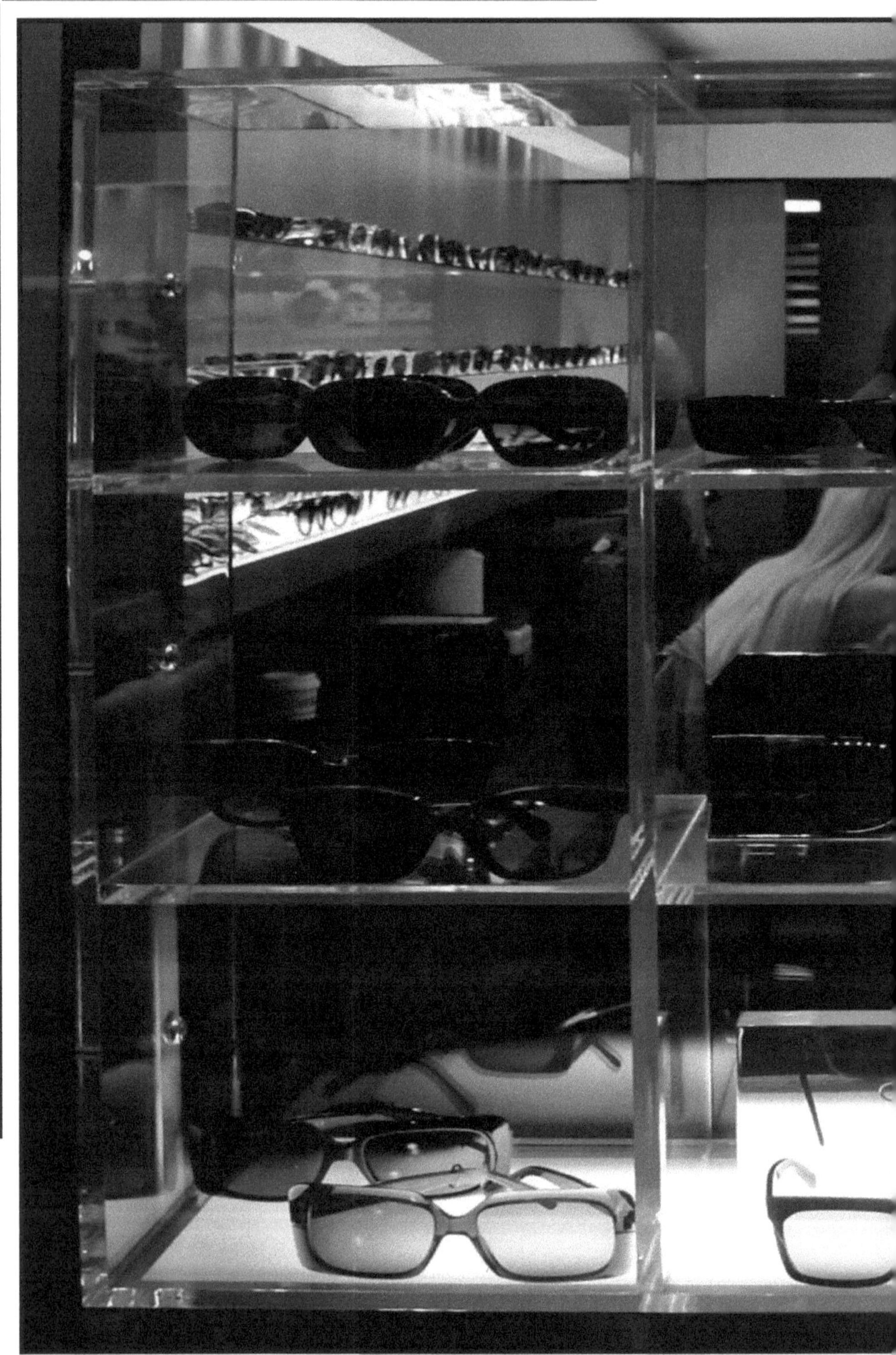

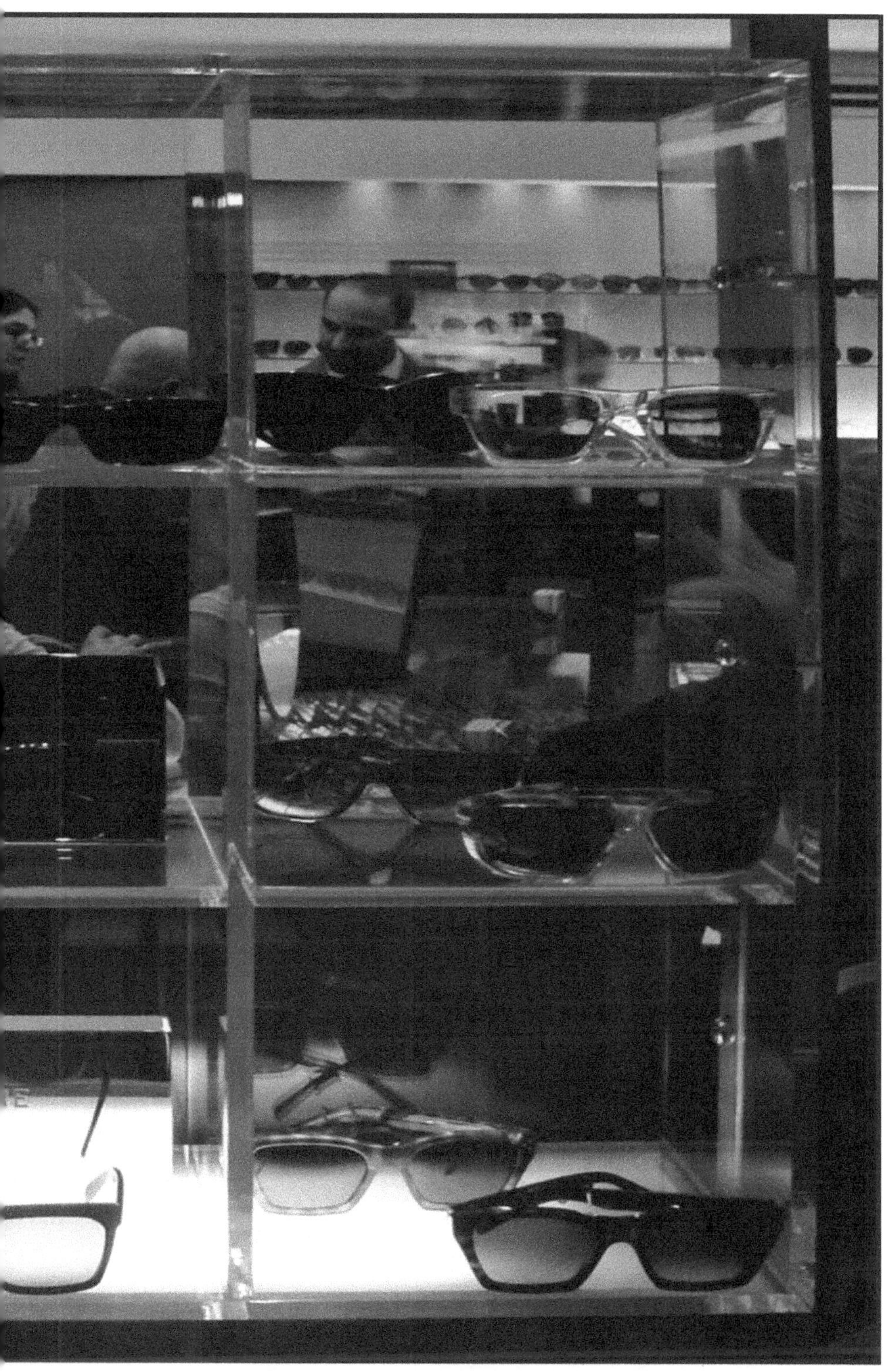

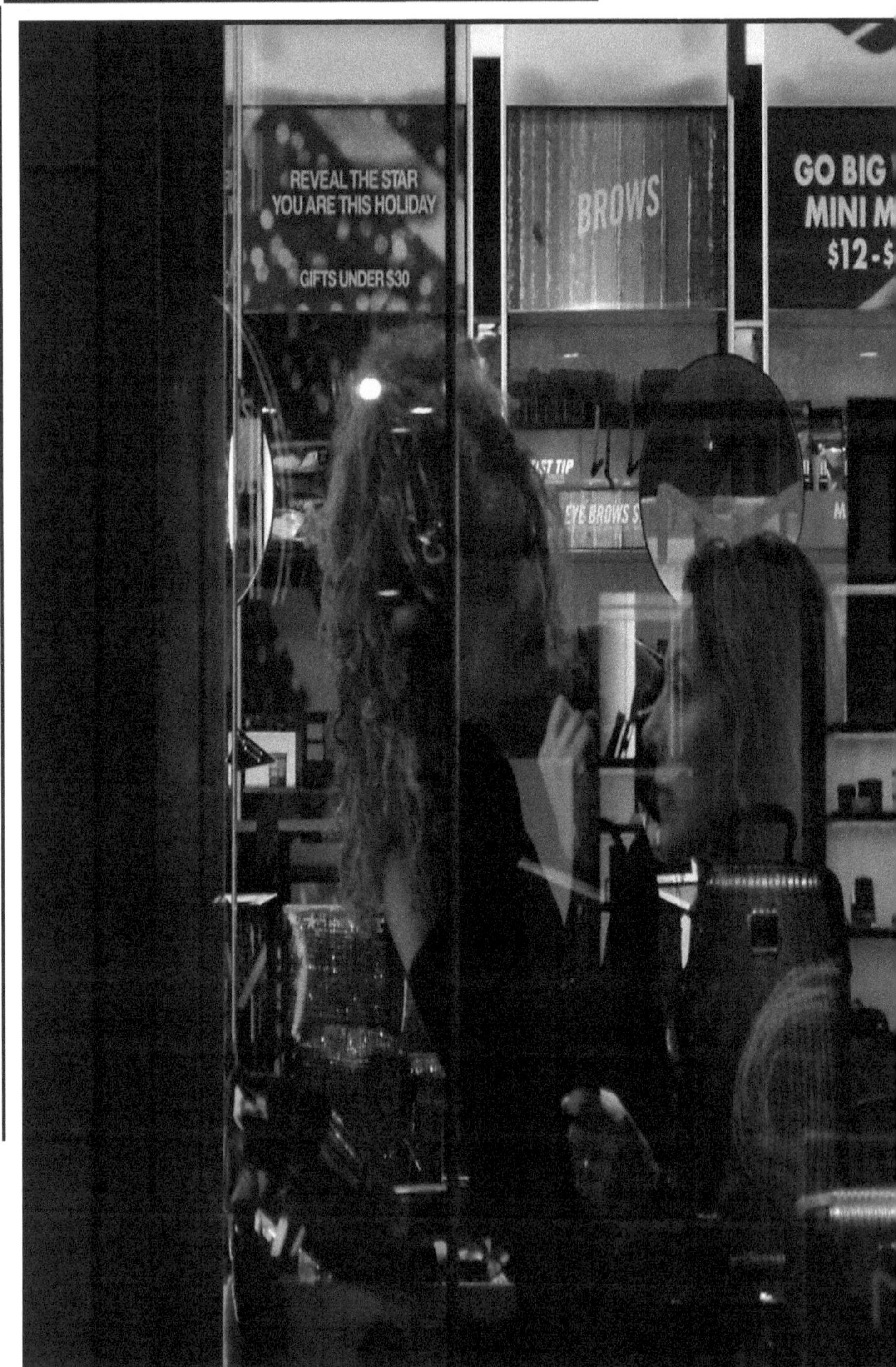

REVEAL THE STAR
YOU ARE THIS HOLIDAY

GIFTS UNDER $30

BROWS

GO BIG
MINI M
$12 - $

EYE BROWS S

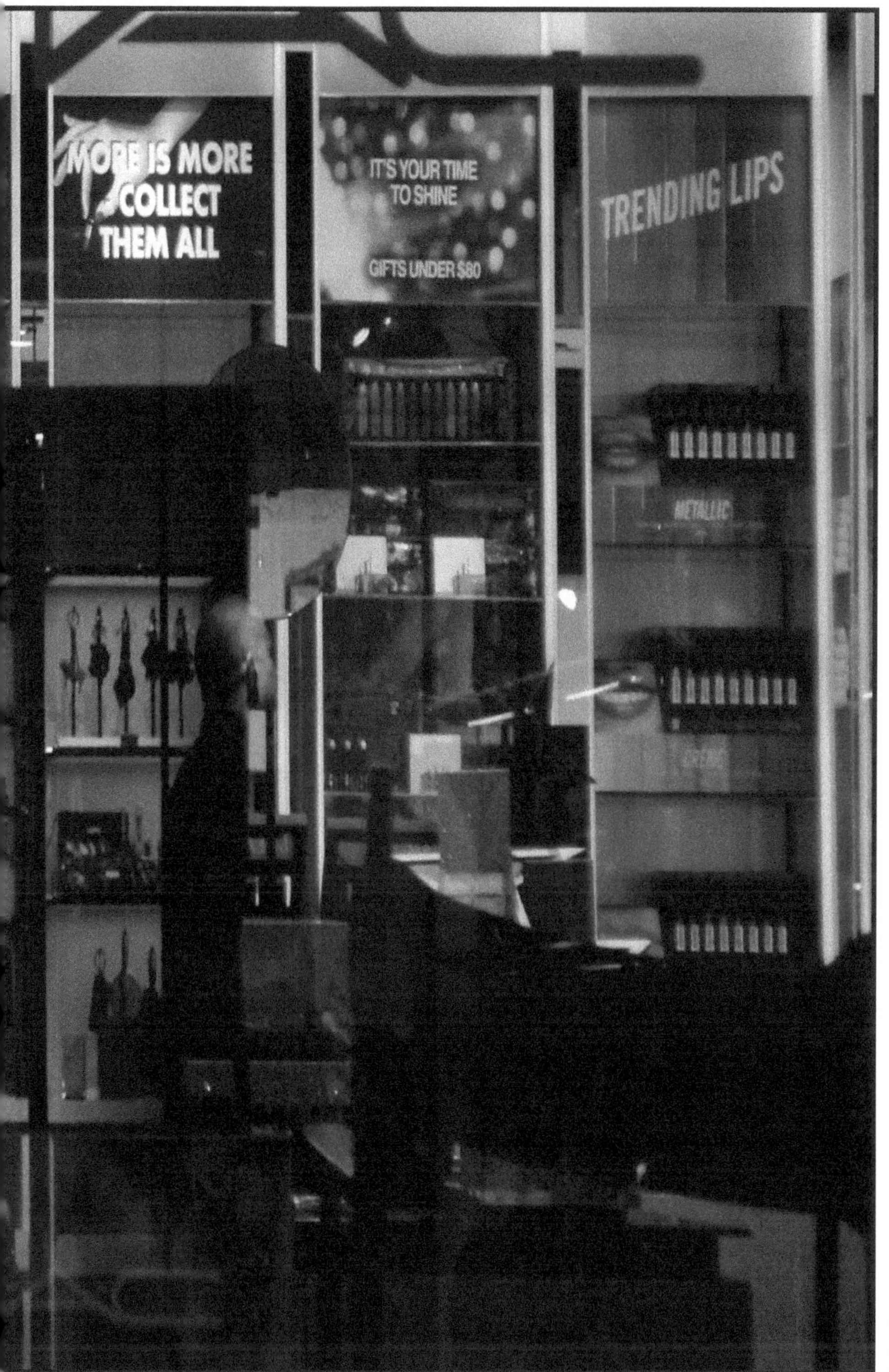

MORE IS MORE
COLLECT
THEM ALL
IT'S YOUR TIME
TO SHINE
GIFTS UNDER $80
TRENDING LIPS
METALLIC
CREME

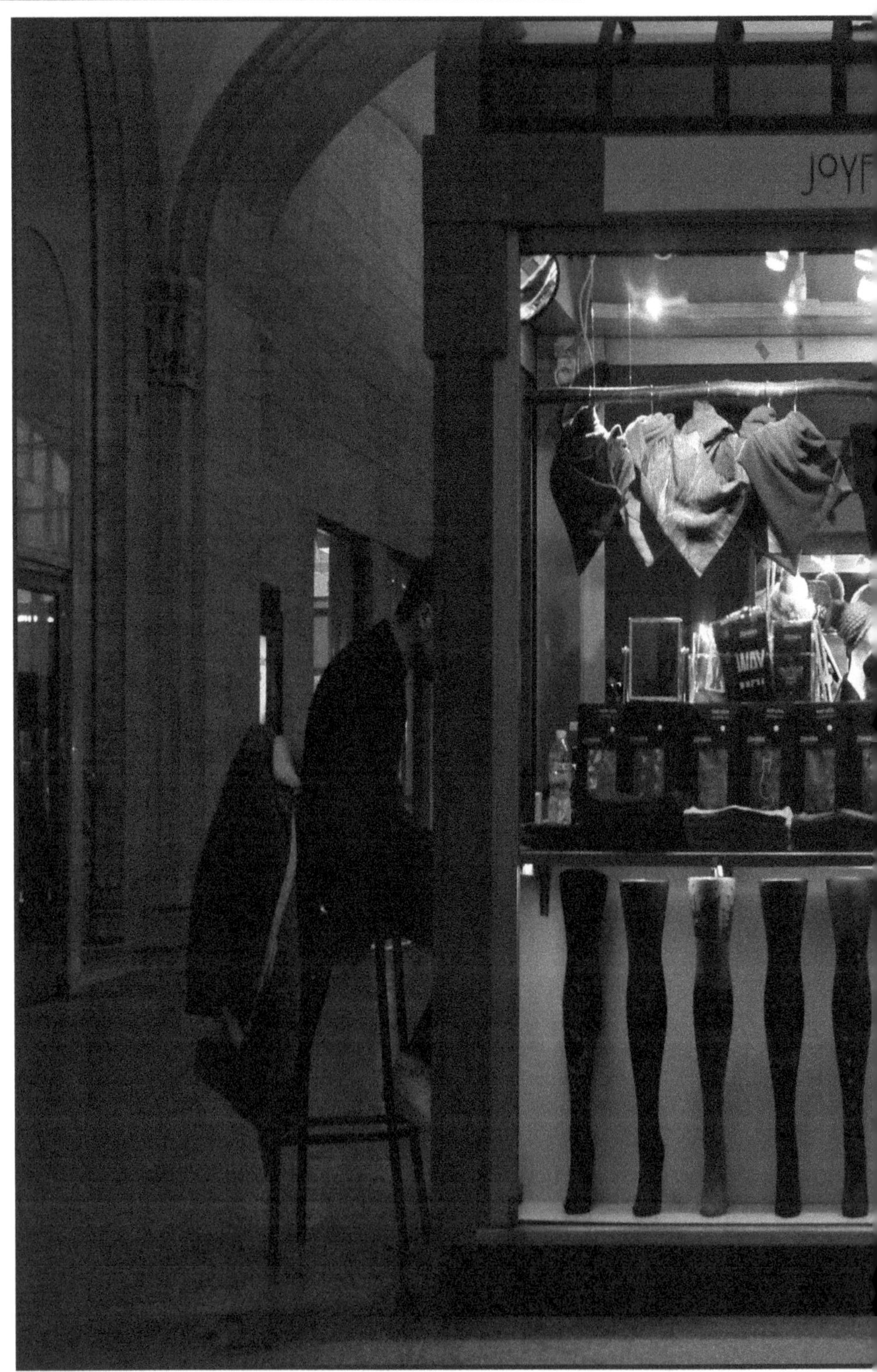

JOYF

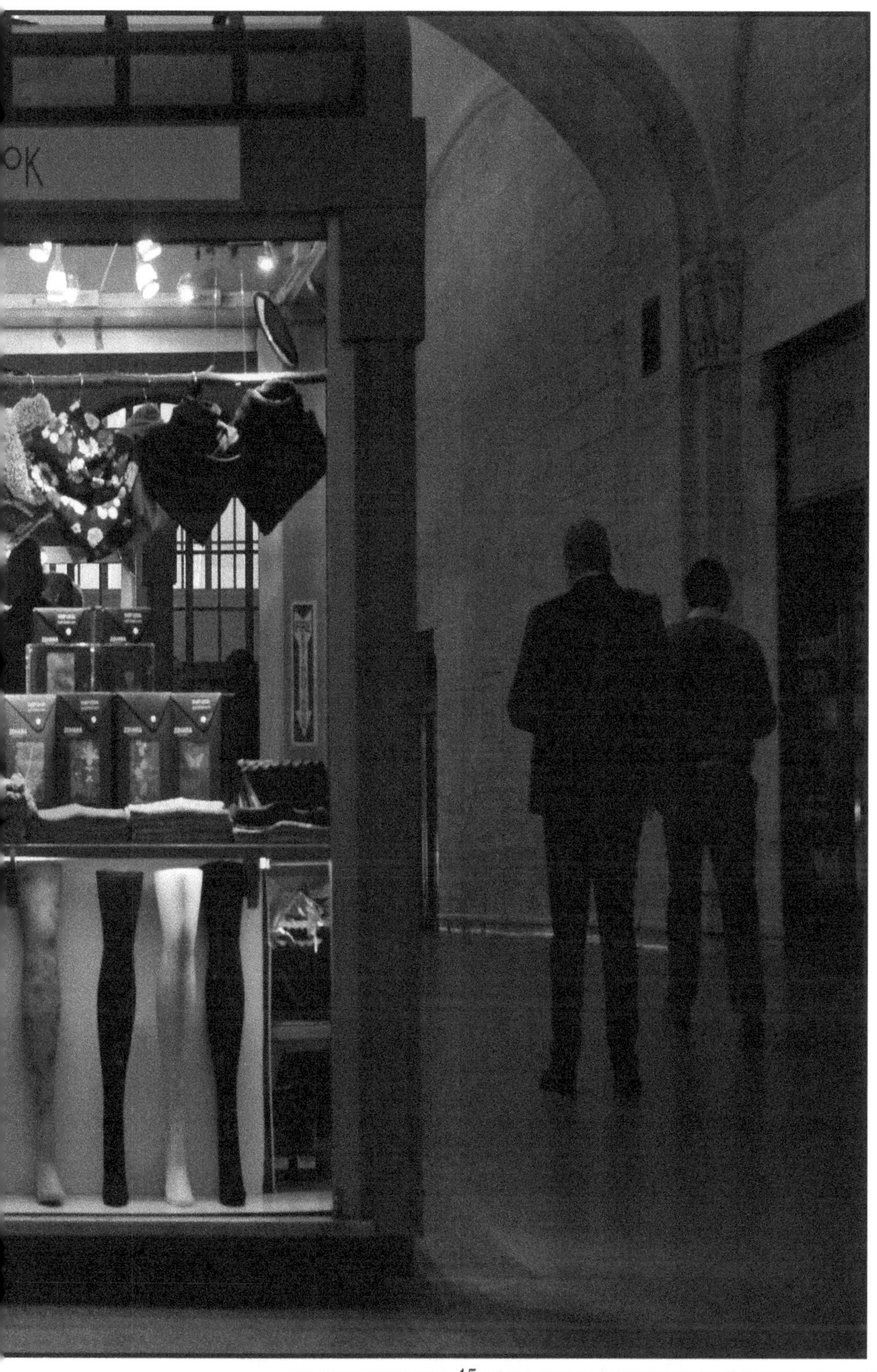

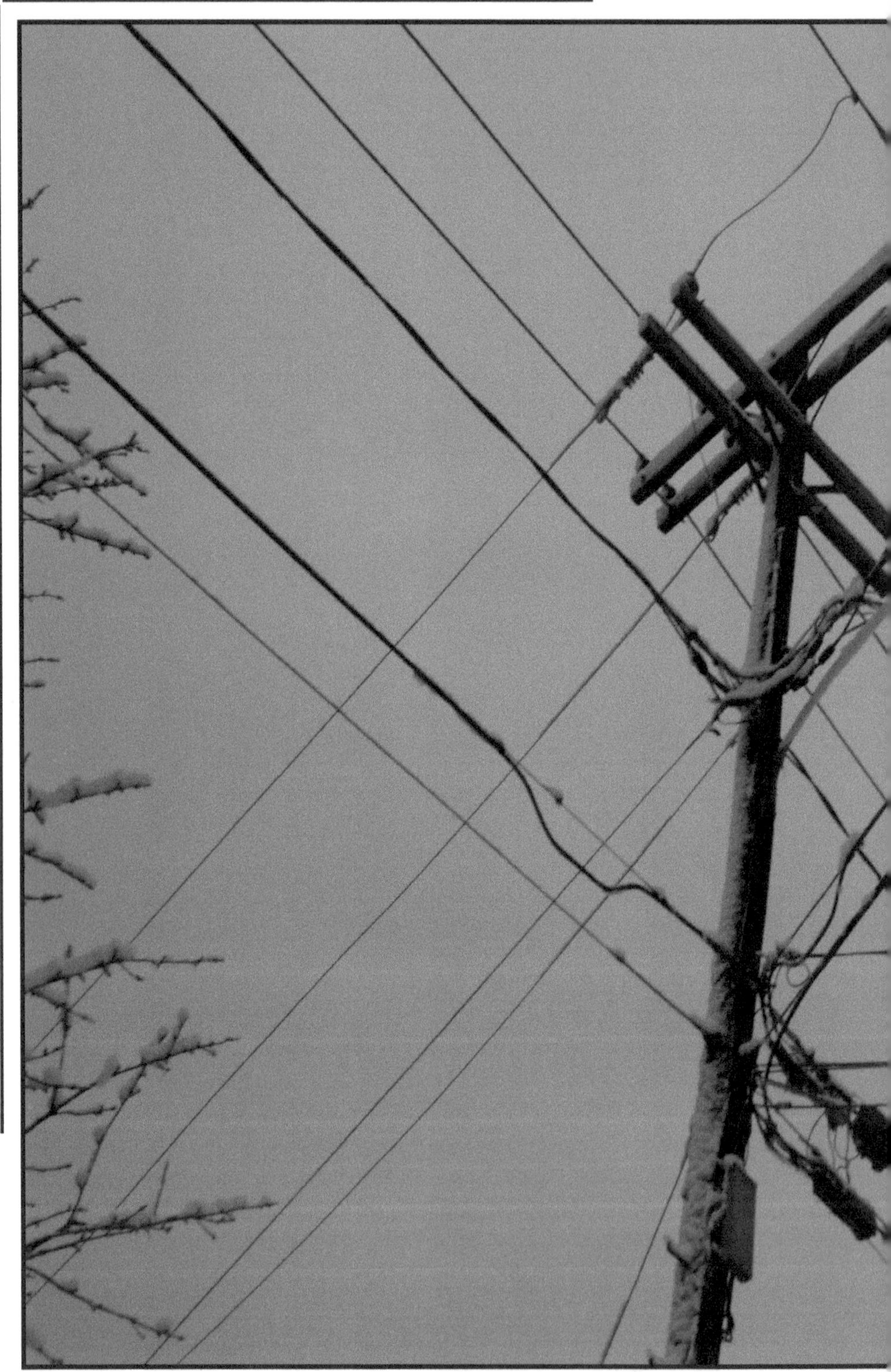

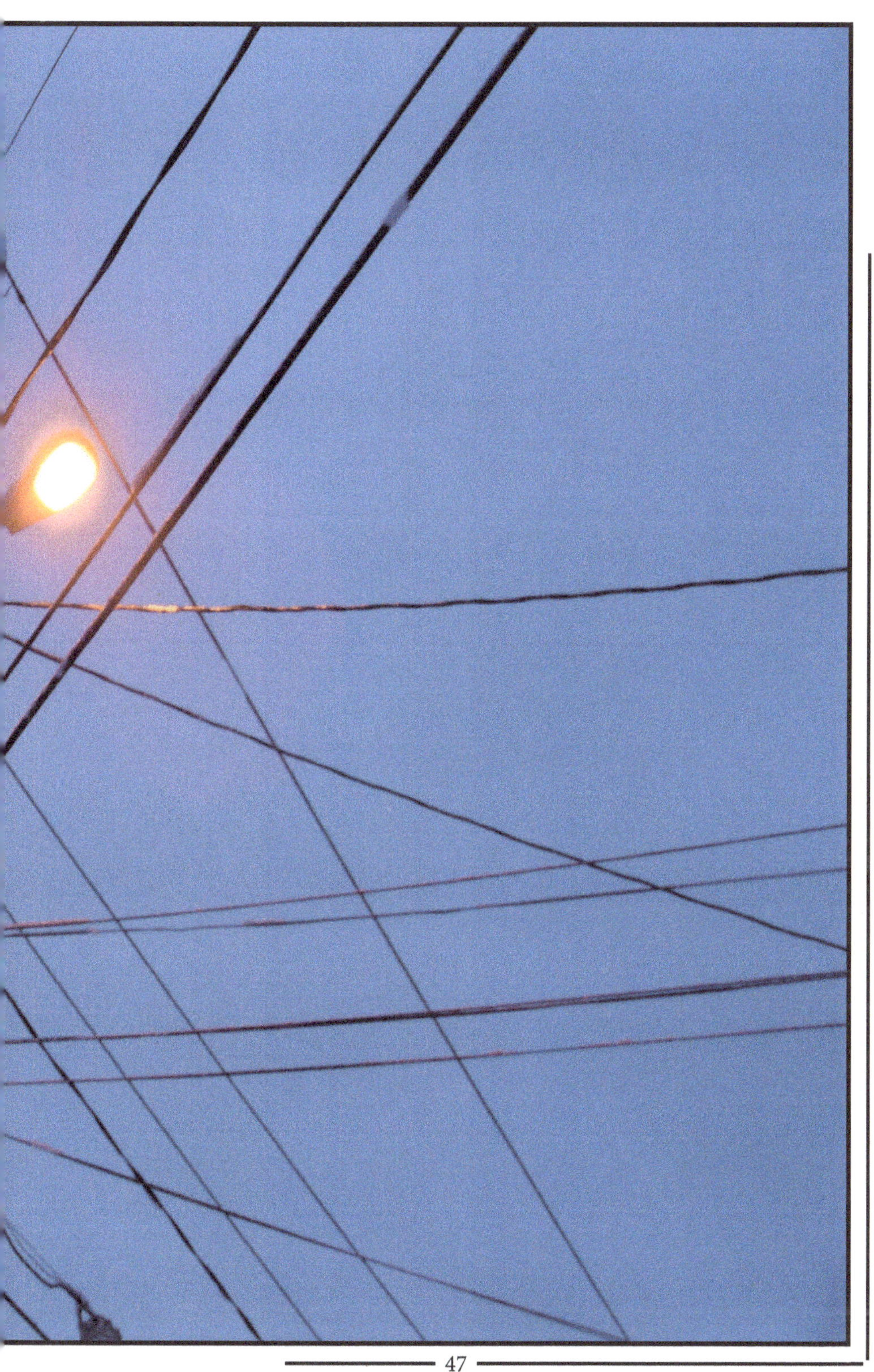

The Inglorious Triumph of Selfishness

Austin Newton

Night descends upon this city
Accosted by a disease
Now holding us hostage.
I mourn the congregations
While roaming these deserted streets,
Moving in and out of each
Neighborhood like hospital rooms
And peeping through windows at
The screens televising this pandemic.

It's been an unholy week;
Death lurks in the spaces between us.
An elderly couple out walking
Seals their fate by holding hands.

I am agent of death
Being outside like this, for
I have touched the sick
And am therefore myself sick.
A man has asked me what time it is;
It's time for me to go home.

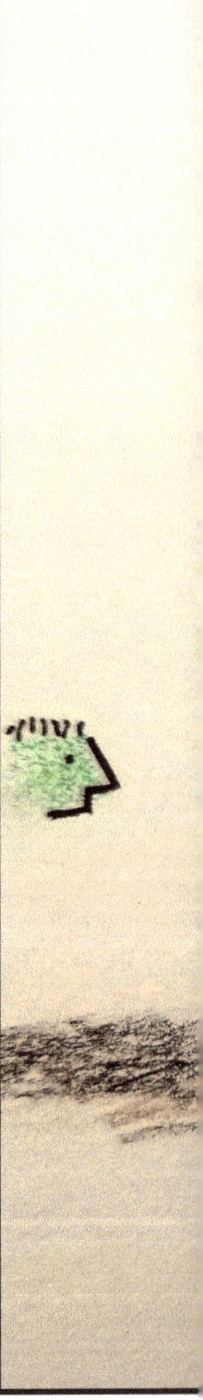

Who are you today?

Bill Schulz

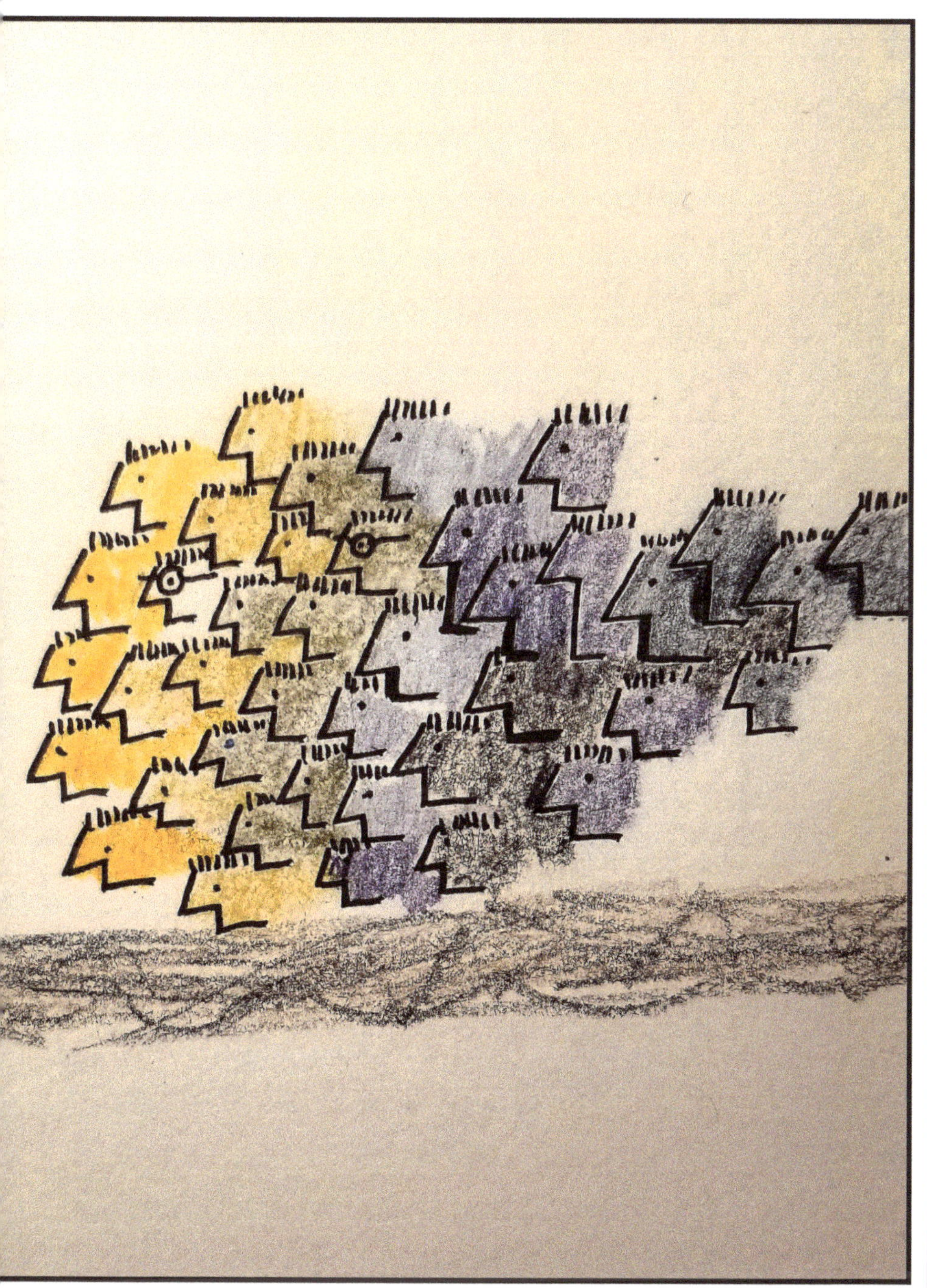

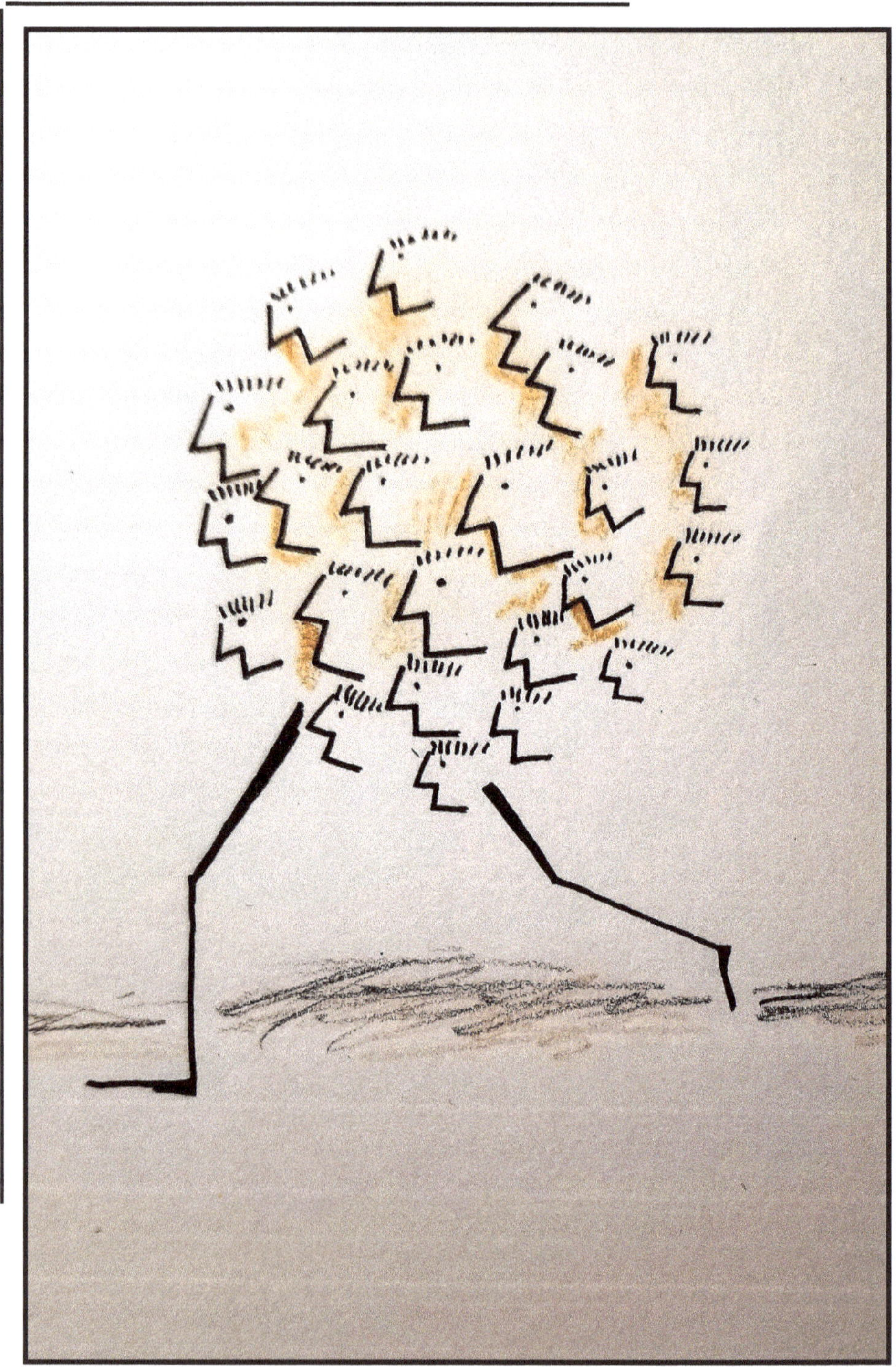

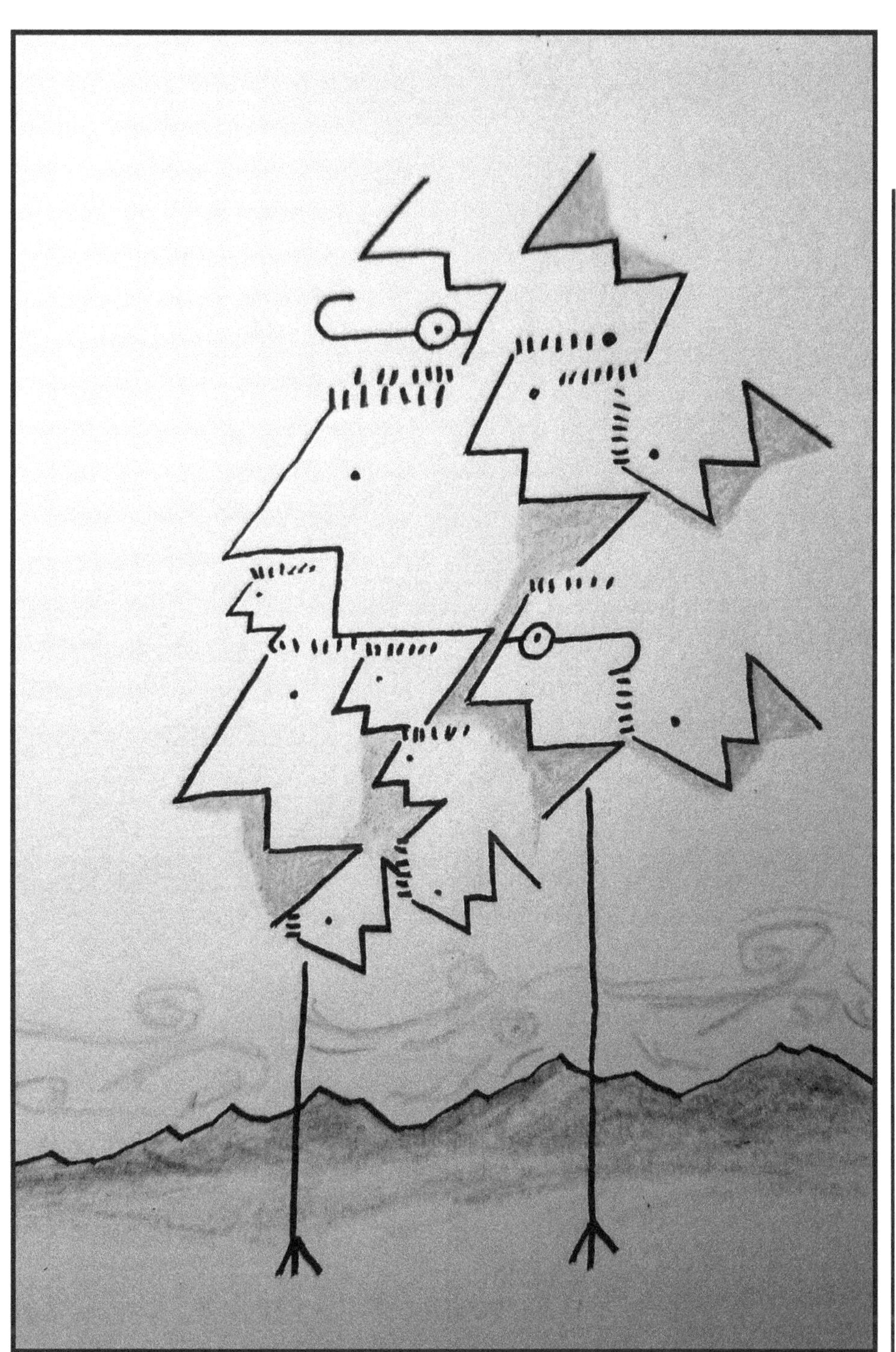

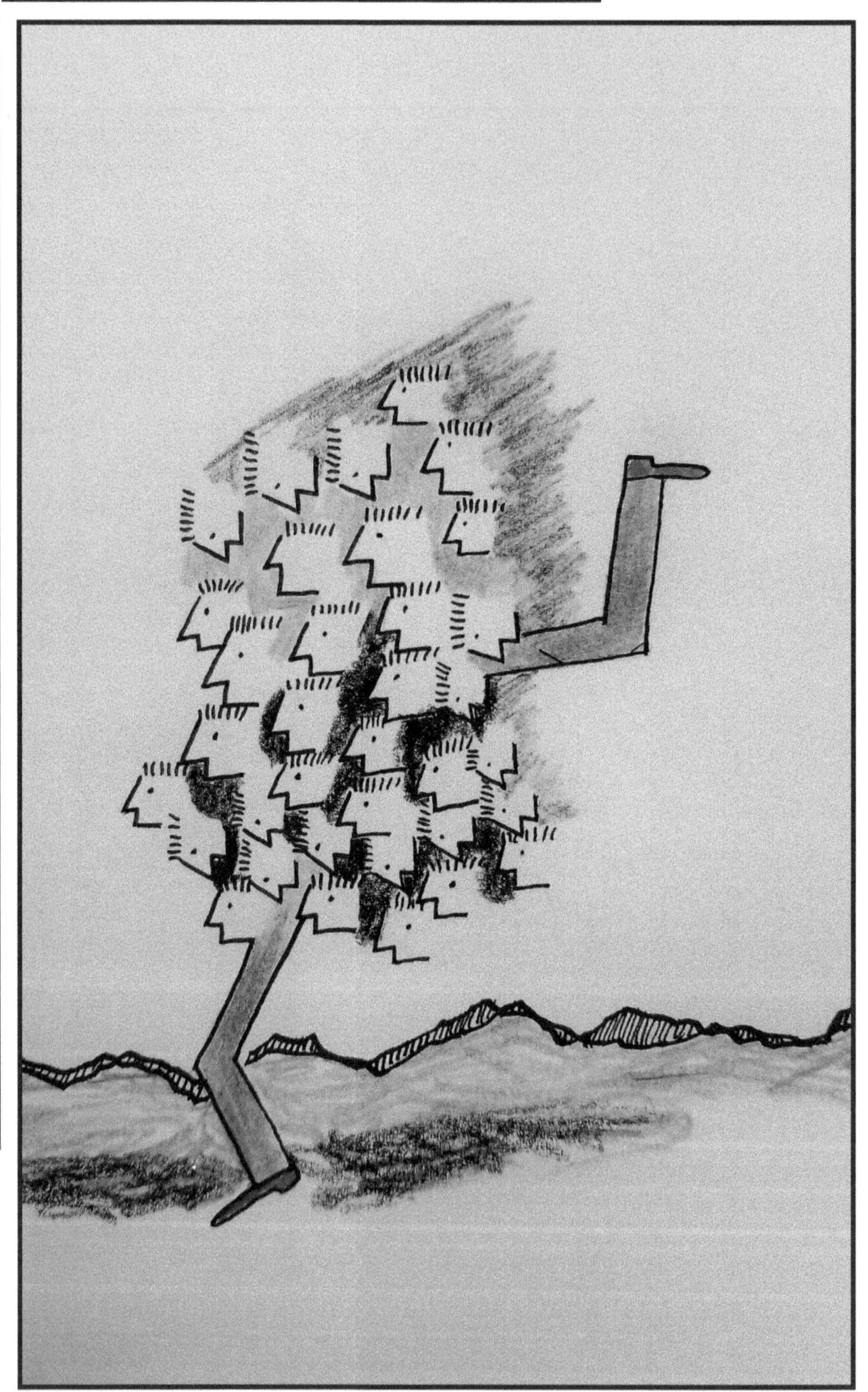

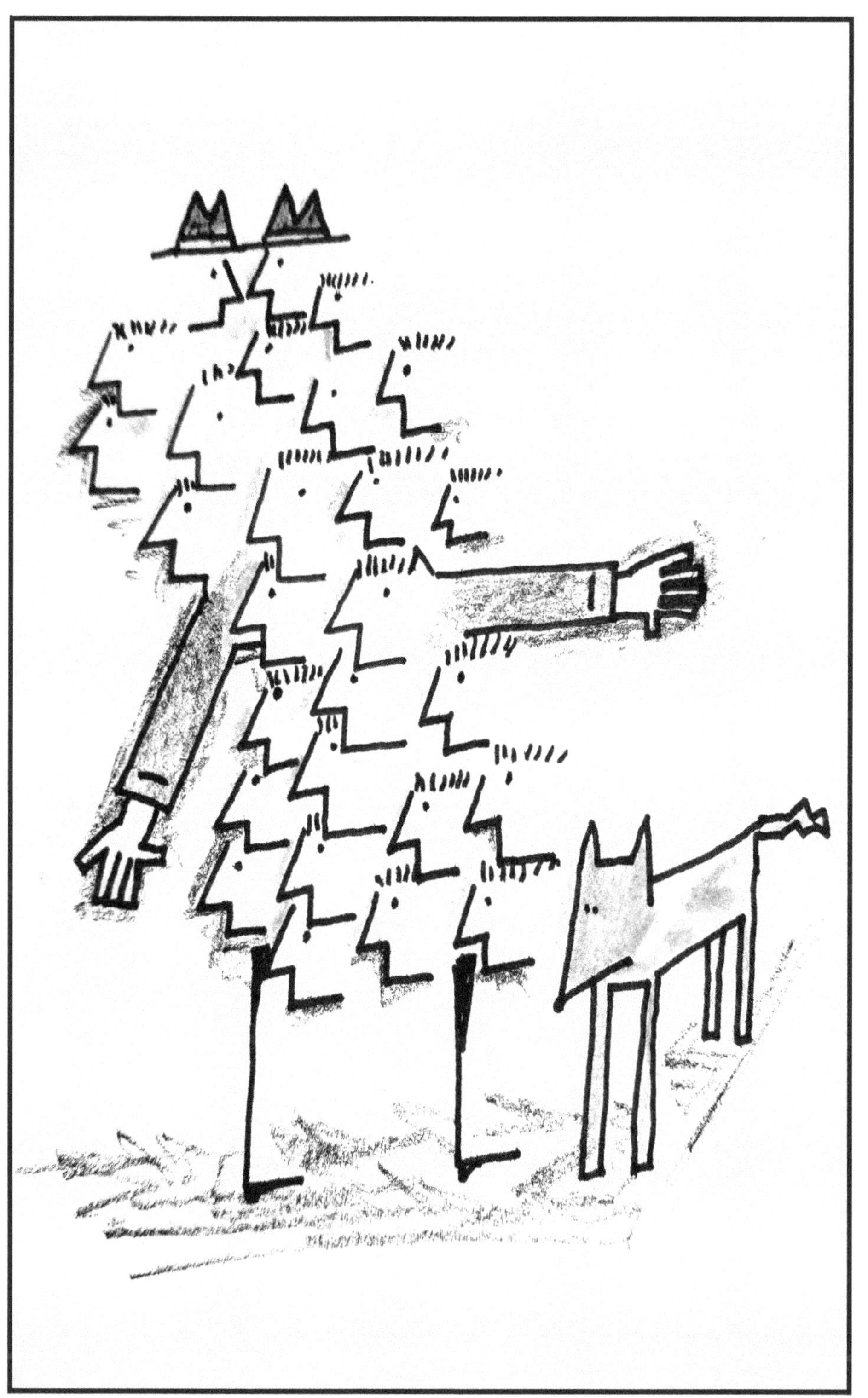

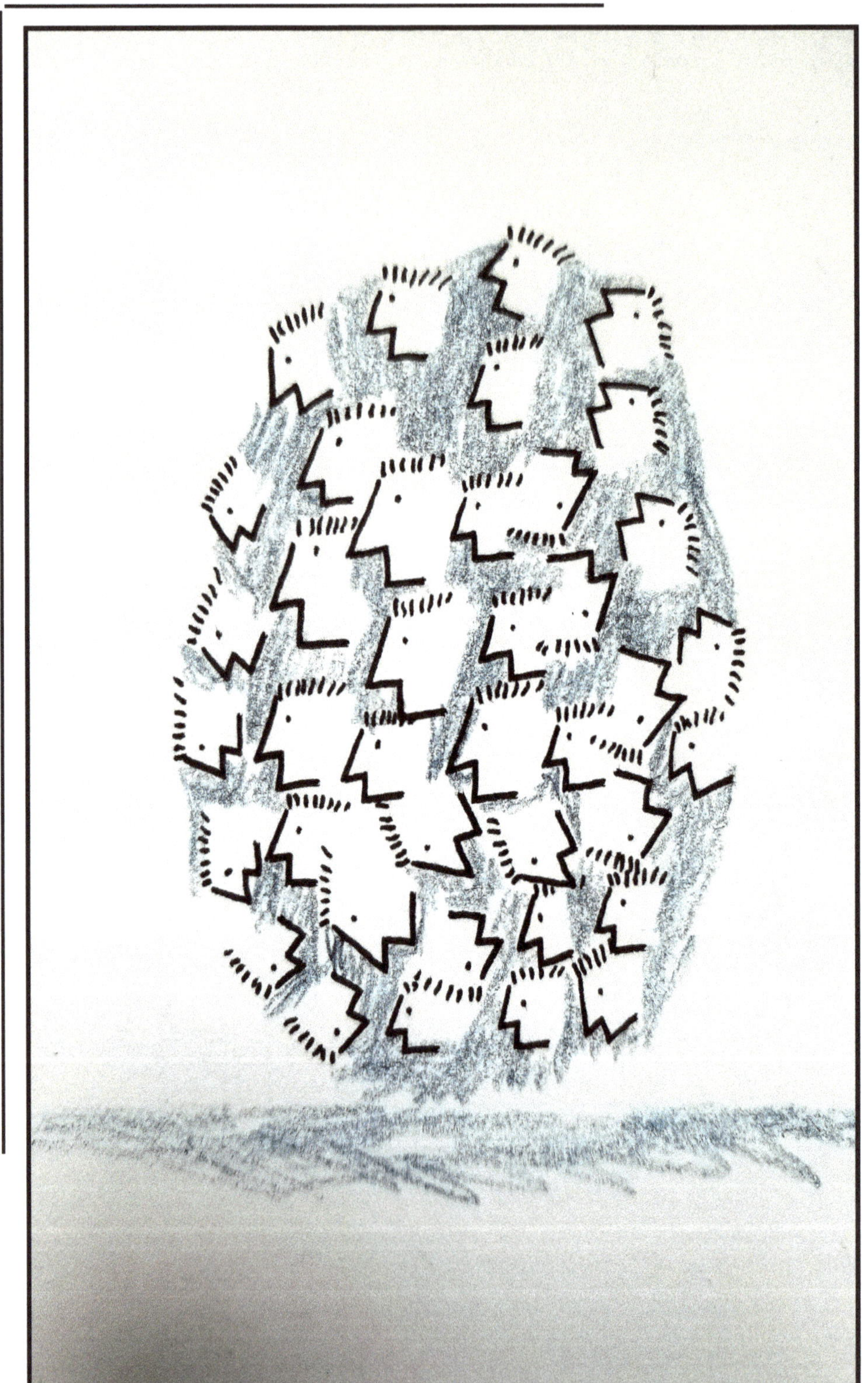

None of them are ours

Hatcher Grey

after Richard Siken

I.
A birthday party. A nest of carpenter bees
under my porch. Tell me our history.
About the dry grits like castrated stingers
on the linoleum floor & tell me the story right
this time. Tell me again
how I'm a weapon in the women's restroom & I'll tell you
about the gun taped under the passenger seat of my first boyfriend's car
& how it did nothing
when he forced his body over mine
like a reflection.
II.
Cigarette burns rise like drowned flies
on the skin of my left arm & I know history.
I lived as a ghost for eighteen years.
I watched as, in his car by the lake,
moths with wings like cellophane
devoured my prom dress.
III.
Tell me again how I'm a brute & I'll tell you
about the boys like me. It's a game like everything else –
who can hold their breath the longest
in the backseat. Put your plastic
cock in my mouth. If your car smells like his perfume
I'll do anything.
IV.
It is my birthday. Tell me again how everyone leaves
eventually. But I'll wait around
until the dead boy who looks like me
stands on a lawn chair,
in the middle of the party
to ask if someone, anyone
will take him home.

lovebug

Connor Thorpe

the sun cracks
and rains in shards
through a grove of
slouching pines

where our bodies bathe
in amber pools
and rest in beds
of stinging nettles

and we take turns
crushing jewelweed
into the welts
that bloom scarlet
across our backs

watching mare's tails
spin endlessly like
a hypnotist's spiral
while we wait for
the sky to burst

our fingers entangled
like lovebugs
until night spills
from a wound
in the blue

and even after all
I've done and
even though the ghost
of my affairs
lives under your skin

you still tilt my head
and help me drink
the last of our wine
from your cupped palm

as every flower in
the garden drones:
something terrible
has happened to us

Mimicry

Charles Kell

How she takes
his hands
turns them over

in the new
November snow.
The white

lighthouse
at the tip
of the window-

less sea
waiting for
the two

to descend—
I kept
wickedness

at bay back
then kept
in my worn

coat's pocket
the photo
from twenty

years ago
keep, now, roaches
locked in

the cupboard
hear their scuttle
as the wind

hits the bricks.
I, like them,
wander

in small circles
nowhere
here my rusty

nail my tin
cup my father's
house

has many
rooms I ran
through once

he is now
dead he
is bones

in the sand
these were
my sister's

hands I tell
you how
I wanted

to be them
tracing
the curves of

my smaller
fingers I love
cold water

how she
dipped them
in salt, touched

each one
with wet strands
of snow-covered

grass

1:21 // rivermourn

Divyasri Krishnan

Further down the bank, the open swell

of tide beneath a new moon. The freshly turned soil
still wet, glistening. Strange beneath

cauterizing light.

I have cut my heels

on these rocks too many times. Here
I might have bled, here, never. Here,

the divots where you dug your feet,

snailshell curve of shying toes, the grit
in the hollows between callouses. Here

I stood again. Felt the moonlight run down

my spine and unwind each tendon with tender
grace. Such loving hands belonged to

no one before. Such kindness never felt, never

spoken. Here, on a smooth stone, the imprint
of a grasping hand. Here, a smear of blood. Always

welcome in the dawn, hallucination, or the making of things

untrue true. Familiar places under new skies. If we
do not recognize the stars, we will, at least, know

this land. Though the night changes,

for a thousand years or two,
we will know these spaces to be true.

Paintings From Rose Cottage: Great Expectations

Lazarus Nazario

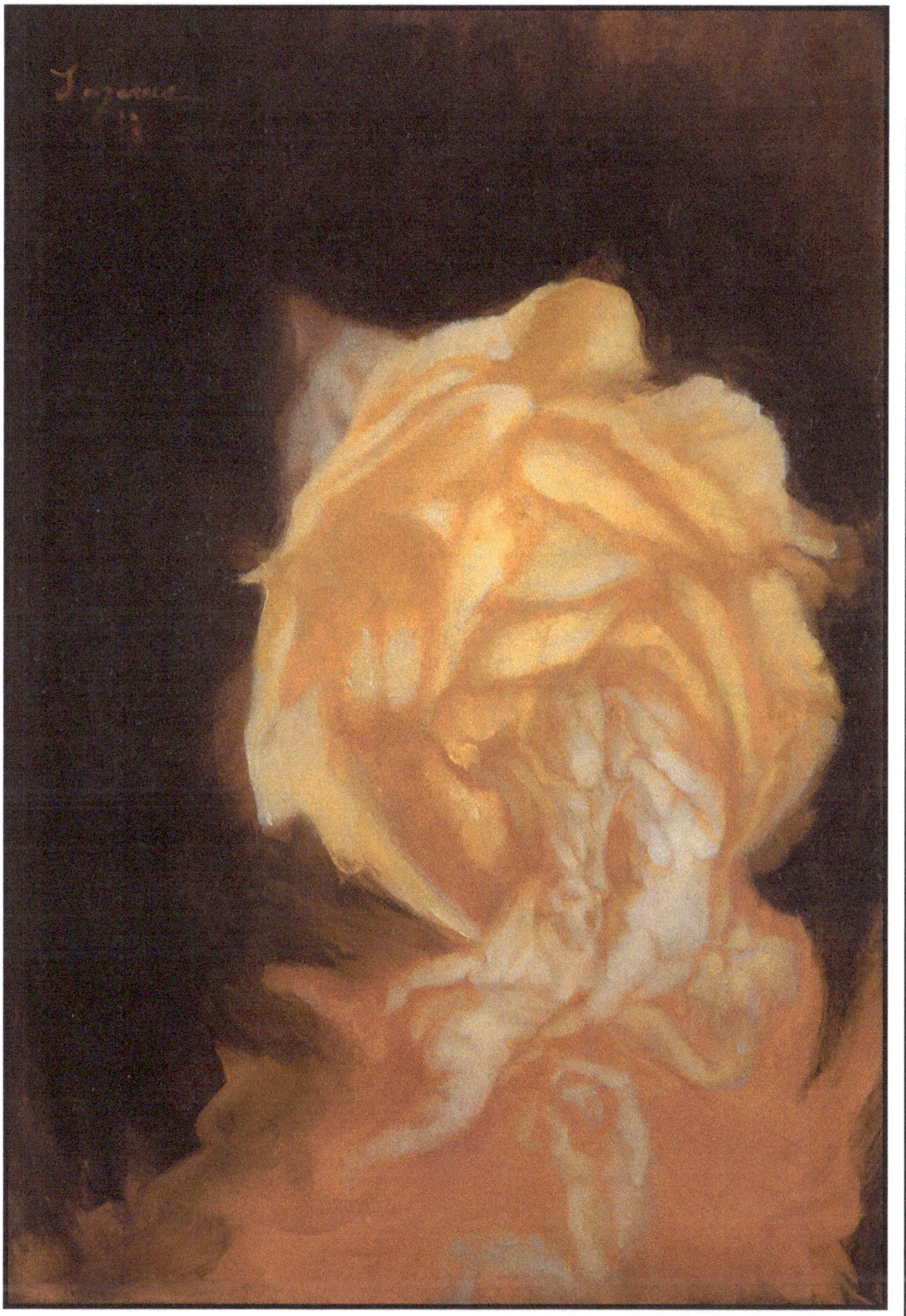

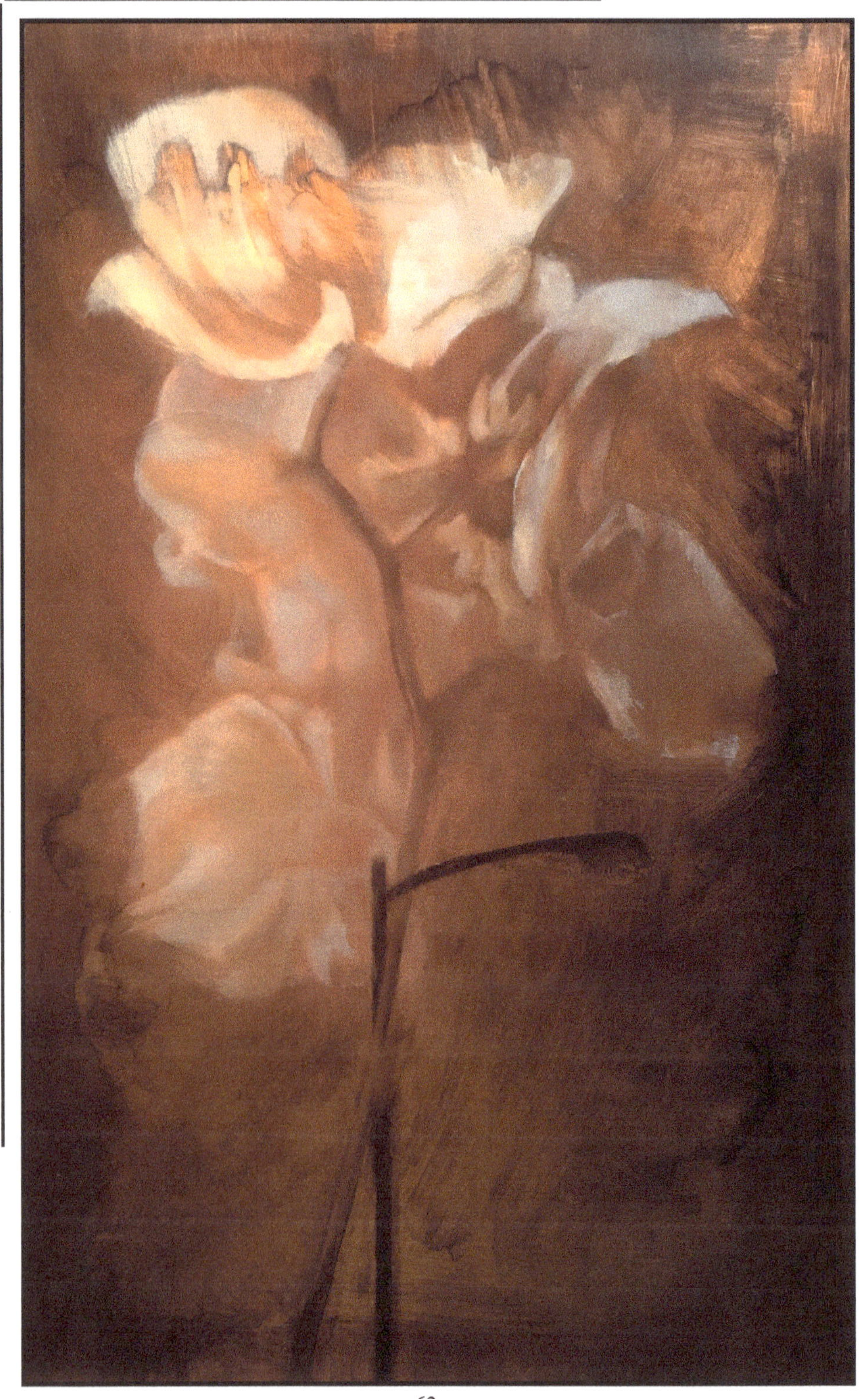

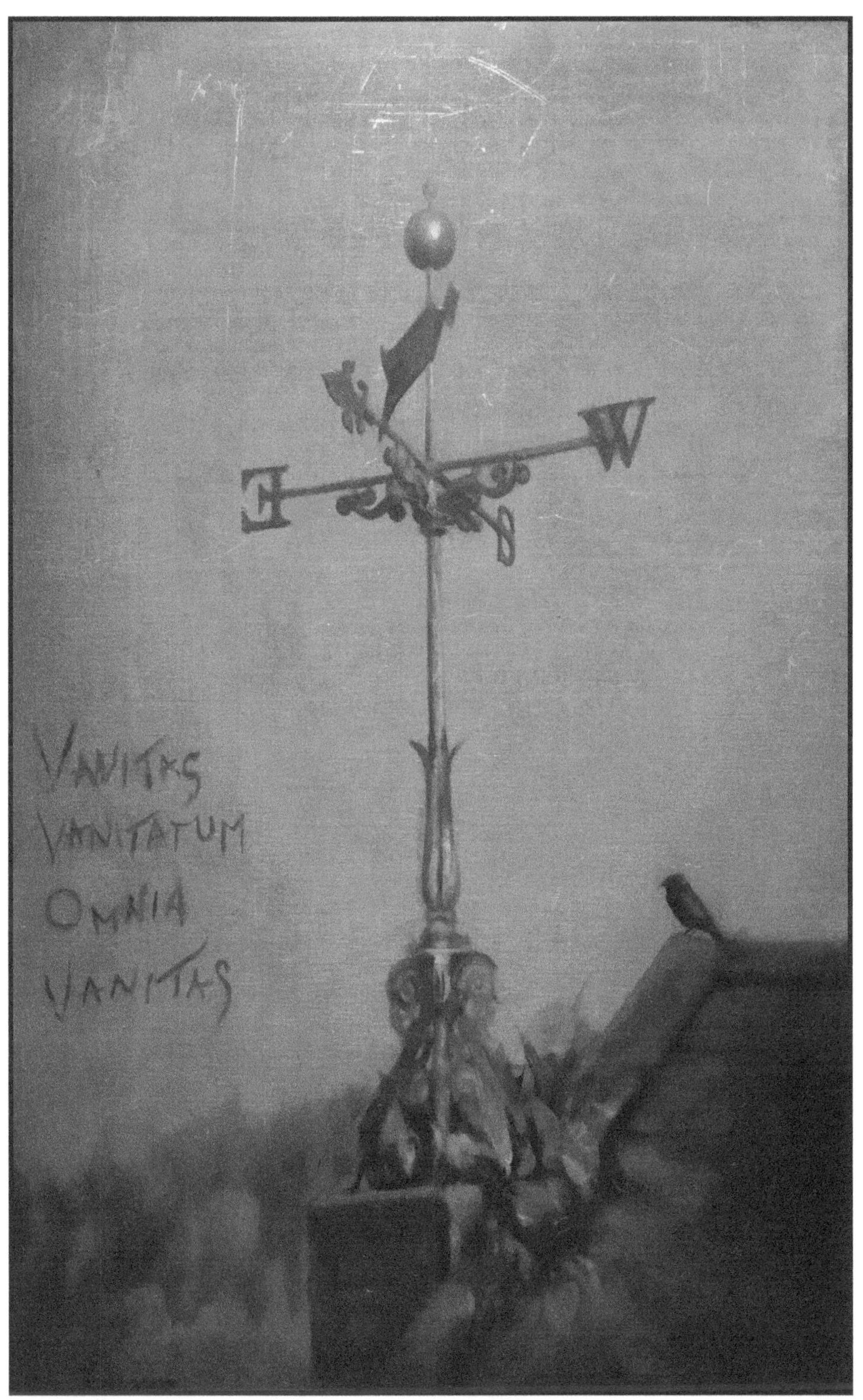

VANITAS
VANITATUM
OMNIA
VANITAS

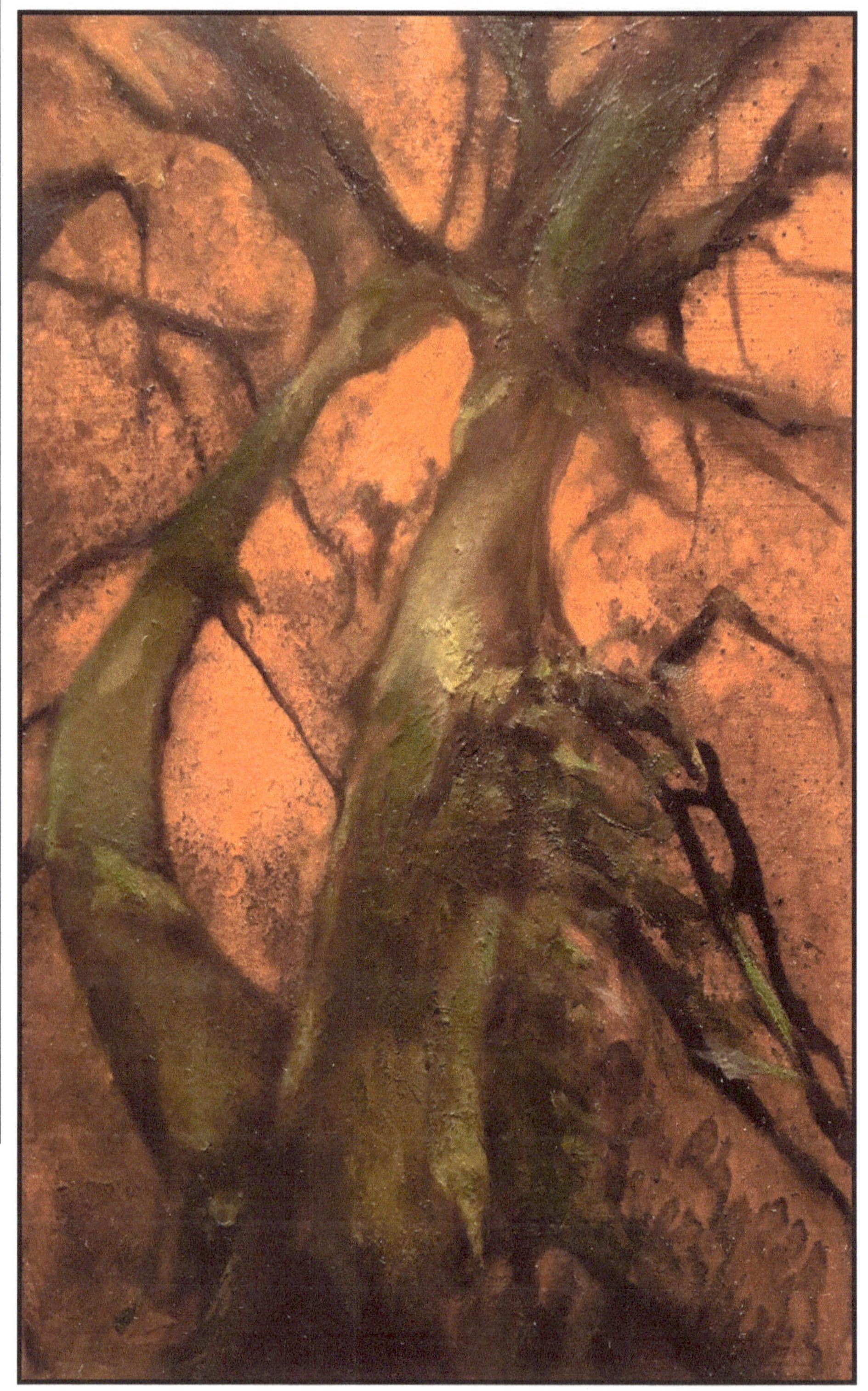

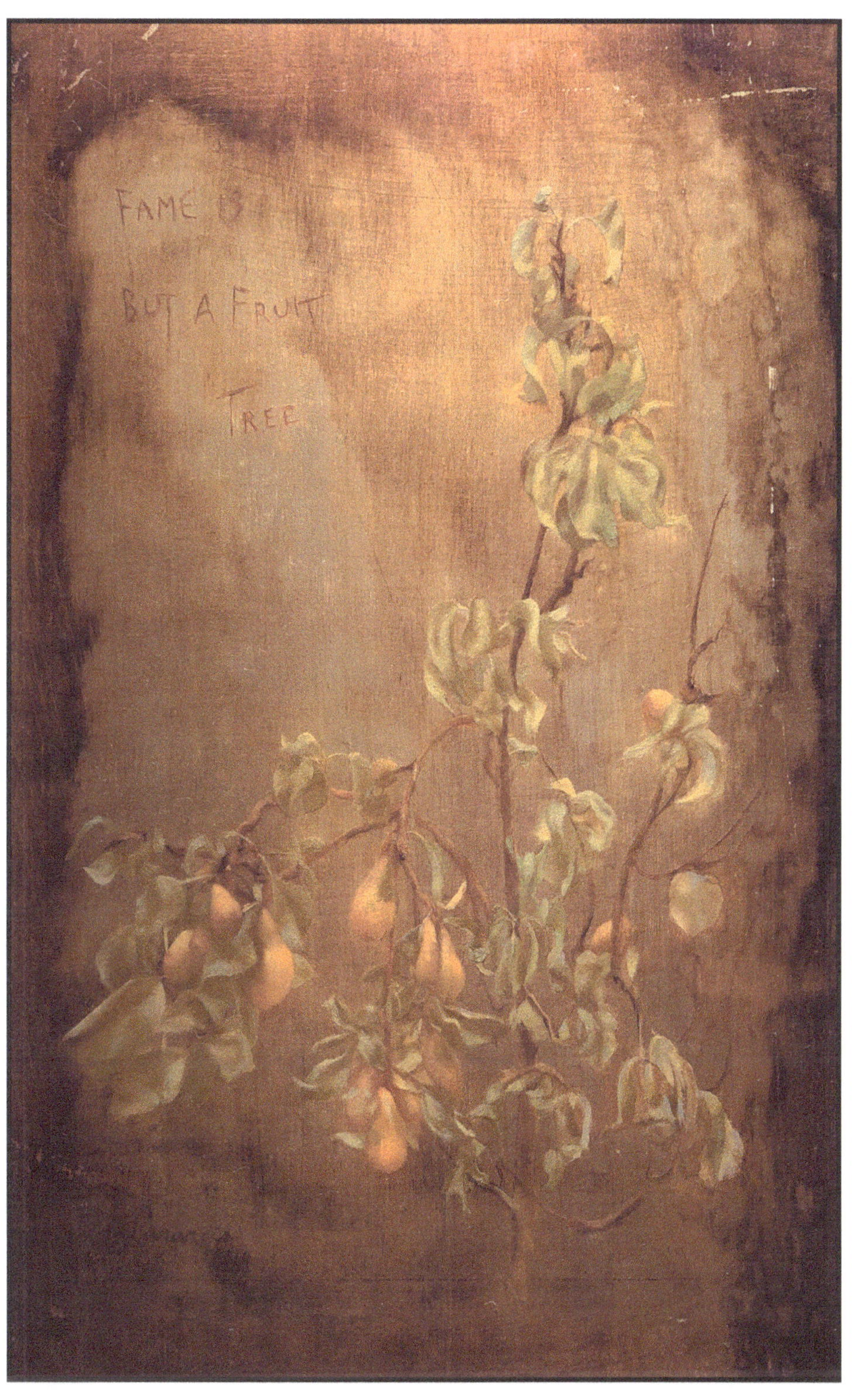
FAME IS
BUT A FRUIT
TREE

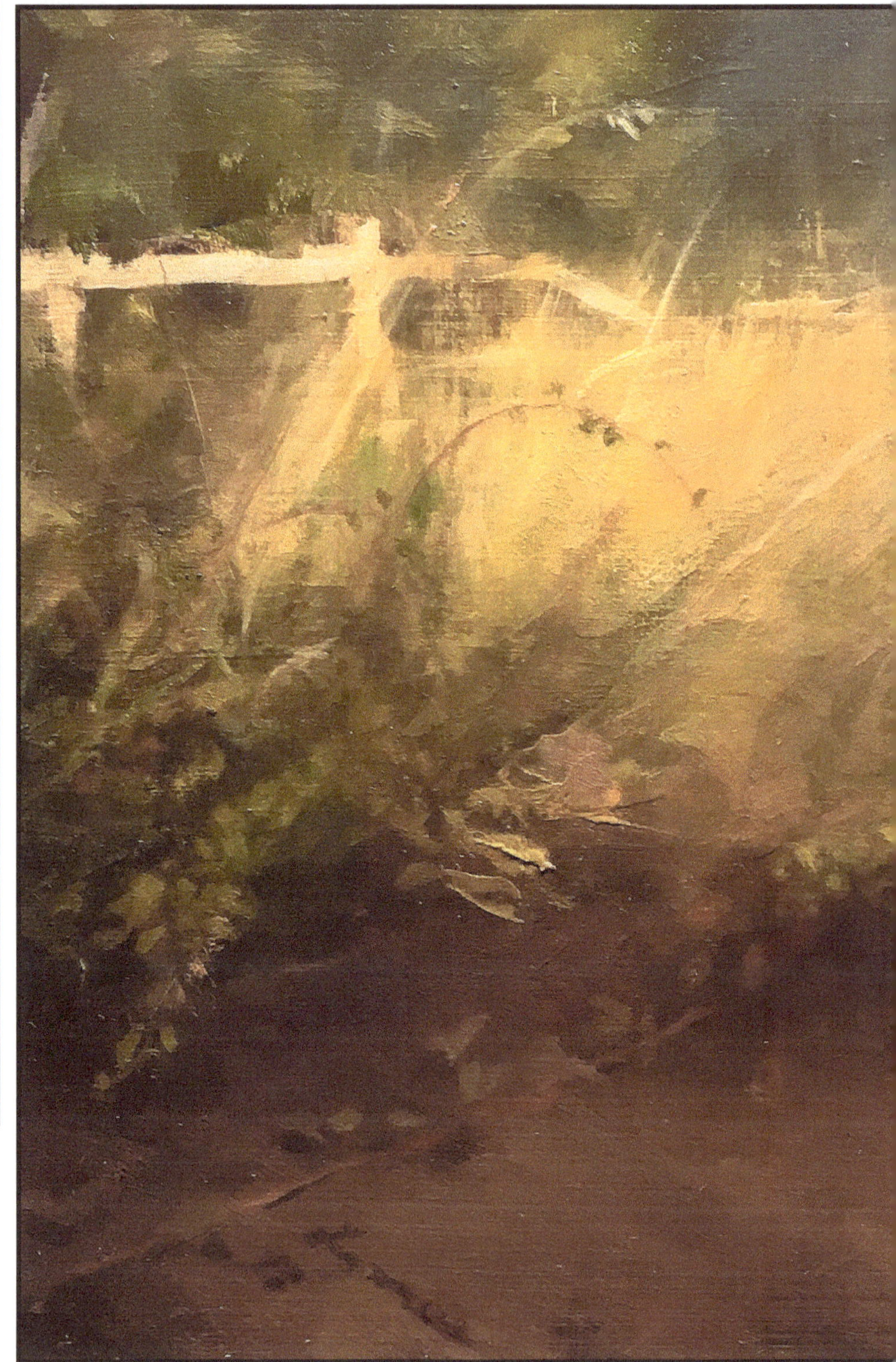

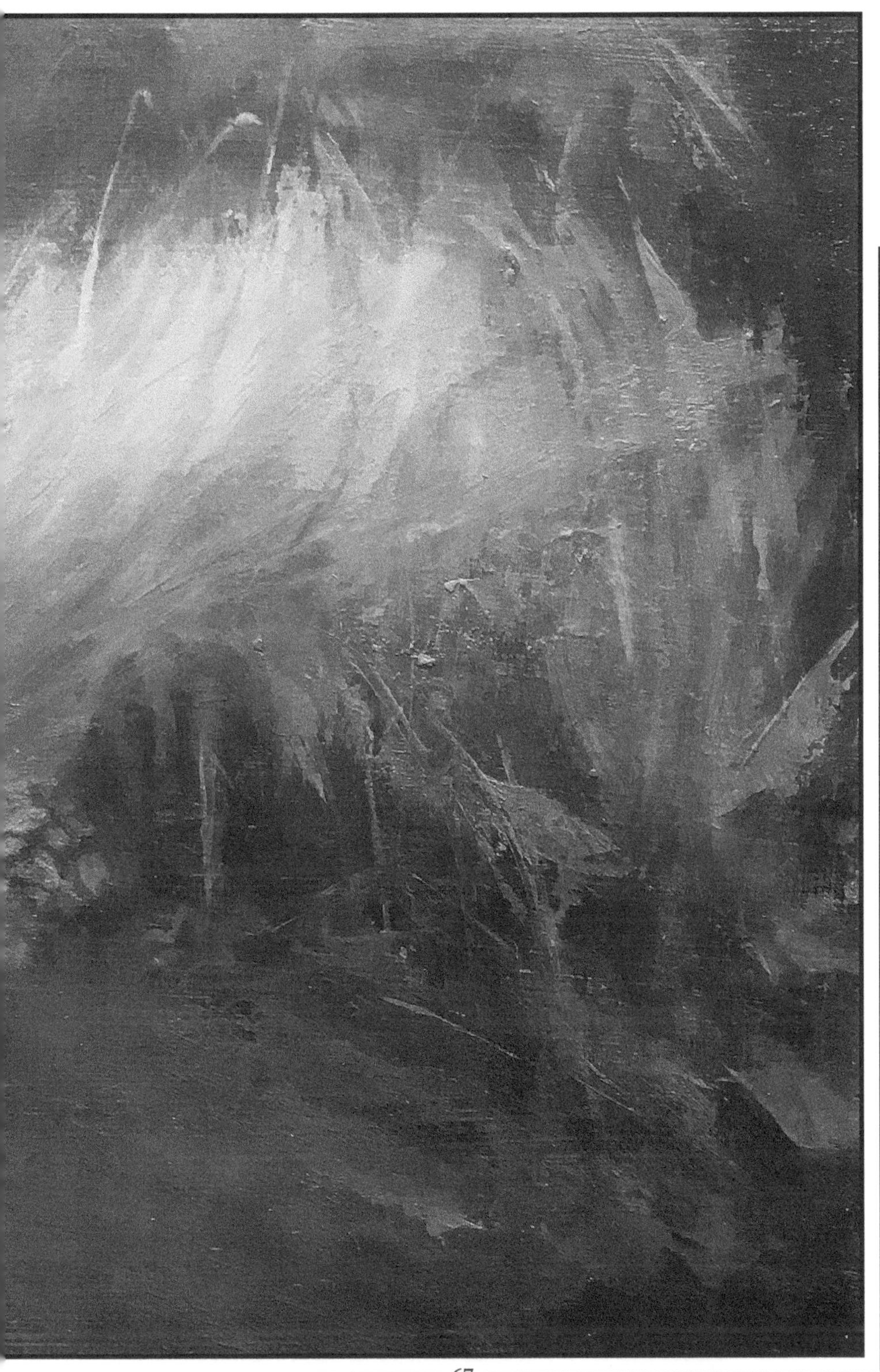

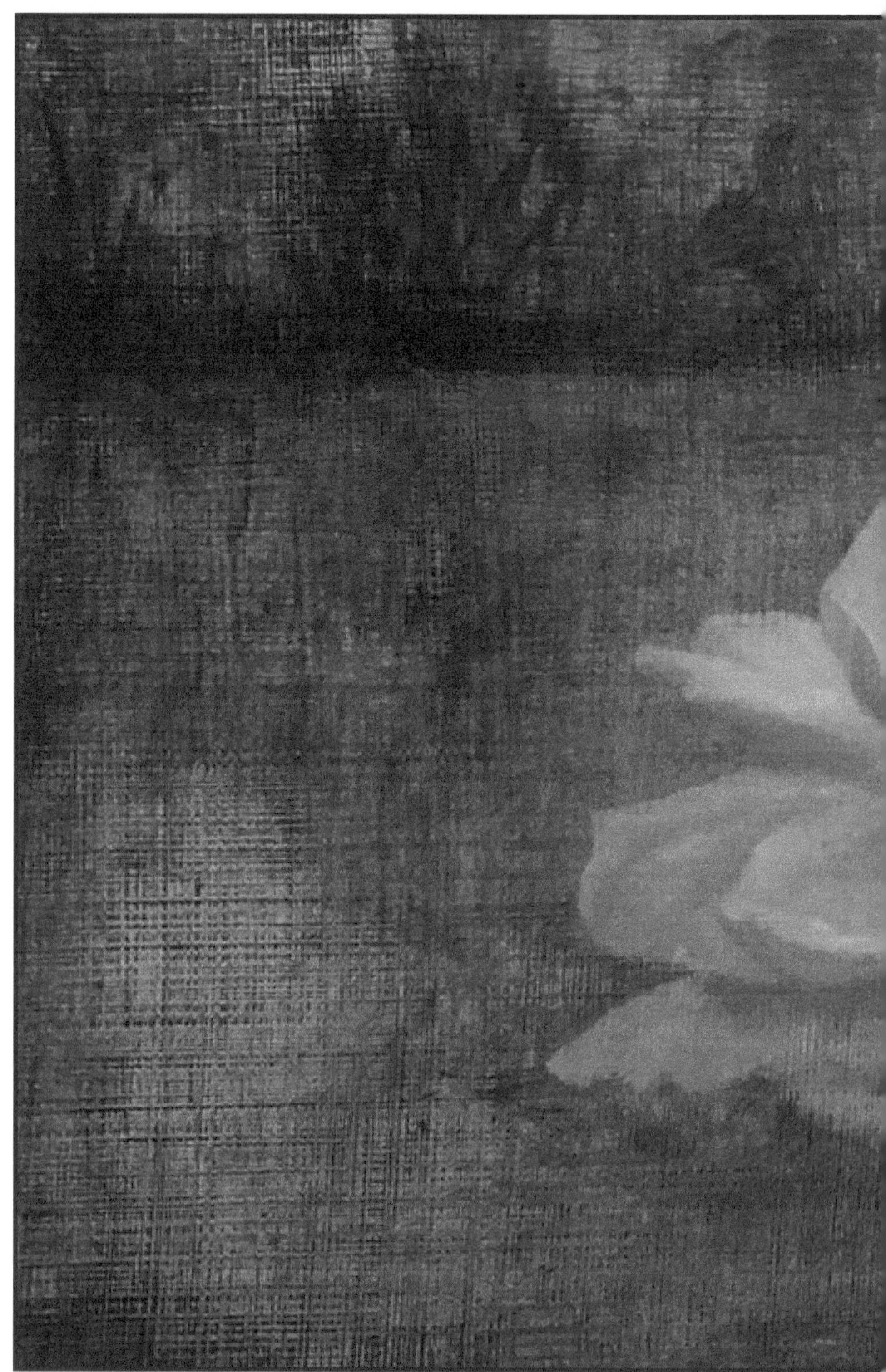

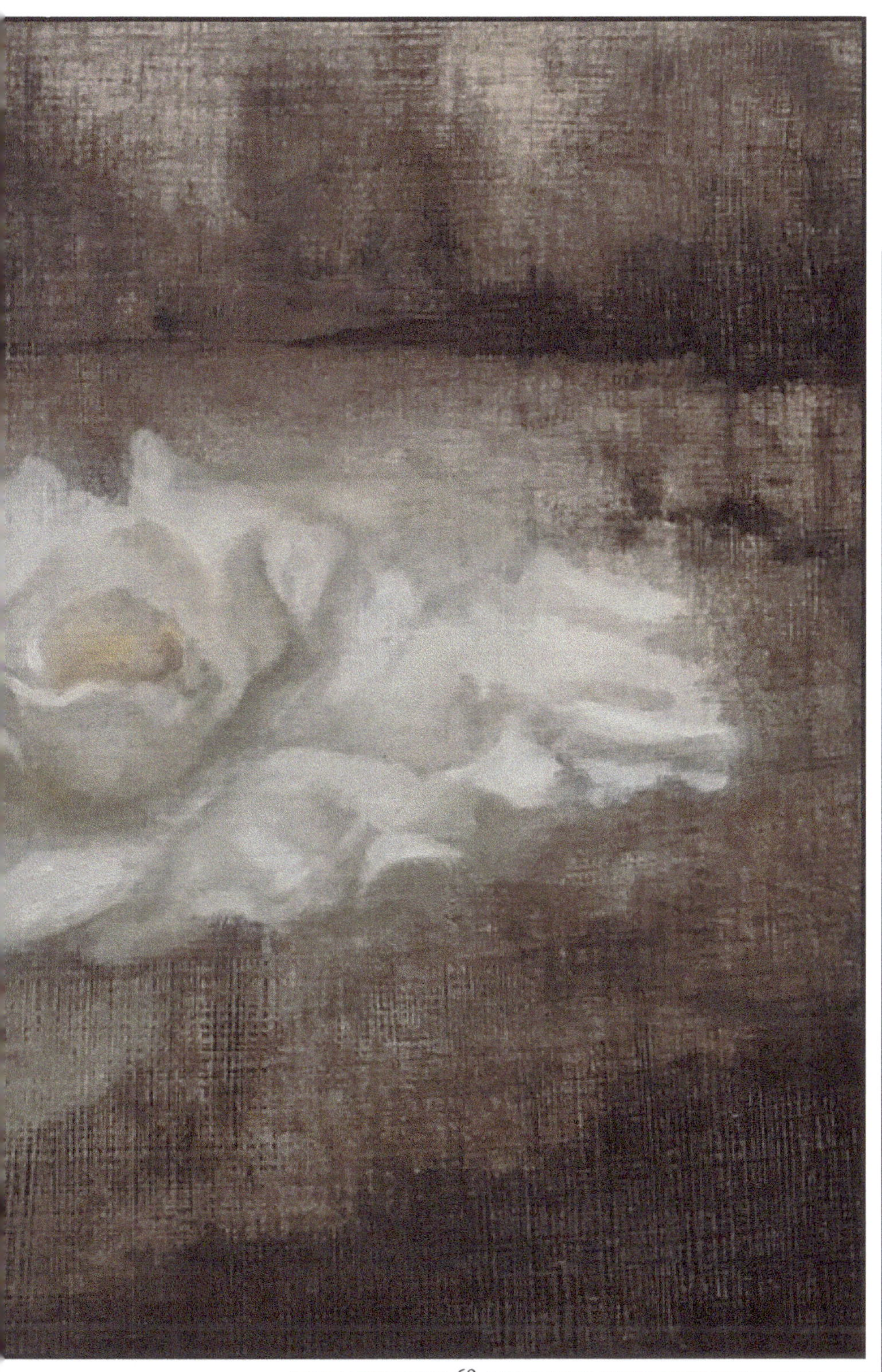

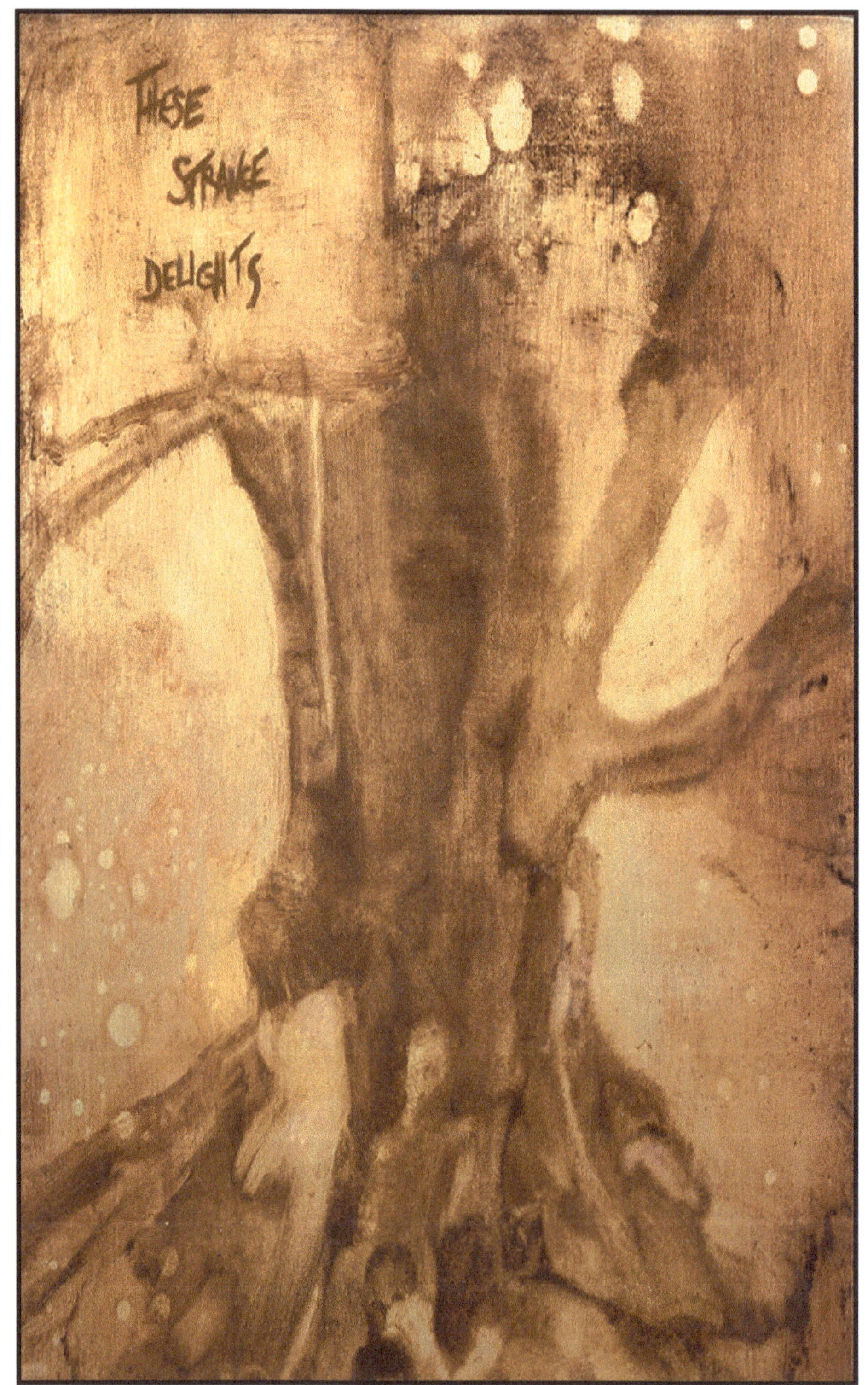

THESE
STRANGE
DELIGHTS

First Urologist Visit: November 14, 2019

Mark Blackford

Tic-Tacs. . .

In a darker time,
a different me allowed myself
to call them by that name

in part due to the beautiful sound they'd make
as they bounced about their plastic bounds
like loose bullets at the bottom of a box,
begging to be chambered and shot into my mouth
but mostly because
like their namesake,
there's no such thing as too many
& you can't have only one.

Nowadays
they go by a more mature name: Ativan.
The label from the pharmacy will read: Lorazepam.
They're being prescribed to me
as an integral part of my vasectomy.
The doctor says they'll ease the tension;
when taken as prescribed,
they will prevent my balls from withdrawing themselves,
making it easier for him
to find and extract the vas deferens
& I get that, because I know

when taken for fun,
benzos have the ability
to melt the brain down like plastic,
press it into a record
play it for the world
and let an imaginary hand
randomly lift the needle.

When the vinyl spins
absent of sound,
you can drive for hours
with your hair caught in a closed window
and not have a fucking clue
before you come to and realize

you're white-knuckling the steering wheel;
the car's in the driveway,
the engine's been running
for god knows how long
& you haven't moved an inch at all.

In large enough quantity,
days deconstruct into dreams
the memory cannot conjure at will
and for those with a mind like mine
such memorably forgettable things
are cherished. I see how this will work;

how my balls will feel better
believing that this is just another
misplaced puzzle piece of a life
I cannot look back on to laugh at;
how I may finally have to explain why
sometimes, I laugh and cry in my sleep.

We get through the formalities,
the doctor and I
& he finally gets to asking me why,
at such a young age,
I want to stop having children.

I feed him some bullshit
about finances
and the state of the world;
how explaining Neo-Nazism
to two toddlers
is enough for one lifetime.
What I neglect to mention
is that this appointment marks
two months of my being sober.
I'm barely 31.

For 17 years of that not a night went by
that I didn't have to put together the next morning.
For 10 of those 17 I've been a partner;
for 6 of those 10 I've been a parent,
and 60 days ago I woke on an empty bed
in clothes I did not remember.
On my phone
a picture of me

swimming in a sea of vomit
& four sentence fragments:
This. Has. To. Stop.

I neglect to mention how, on that day, I gave up
chasing lost puzzle pieces of dreams
& promised to never let anyone down, again;
how that starts right here, with him,
stopping me
from being able to make anyone else, ever
feel that ashamed of me again.

He tells me it could take up to a year
before I am completely sterile

& all I can manage to ask him
is how much longer will I have to wait
until I'm fixed.

If These Walls Could Talk

Sara DiDonato

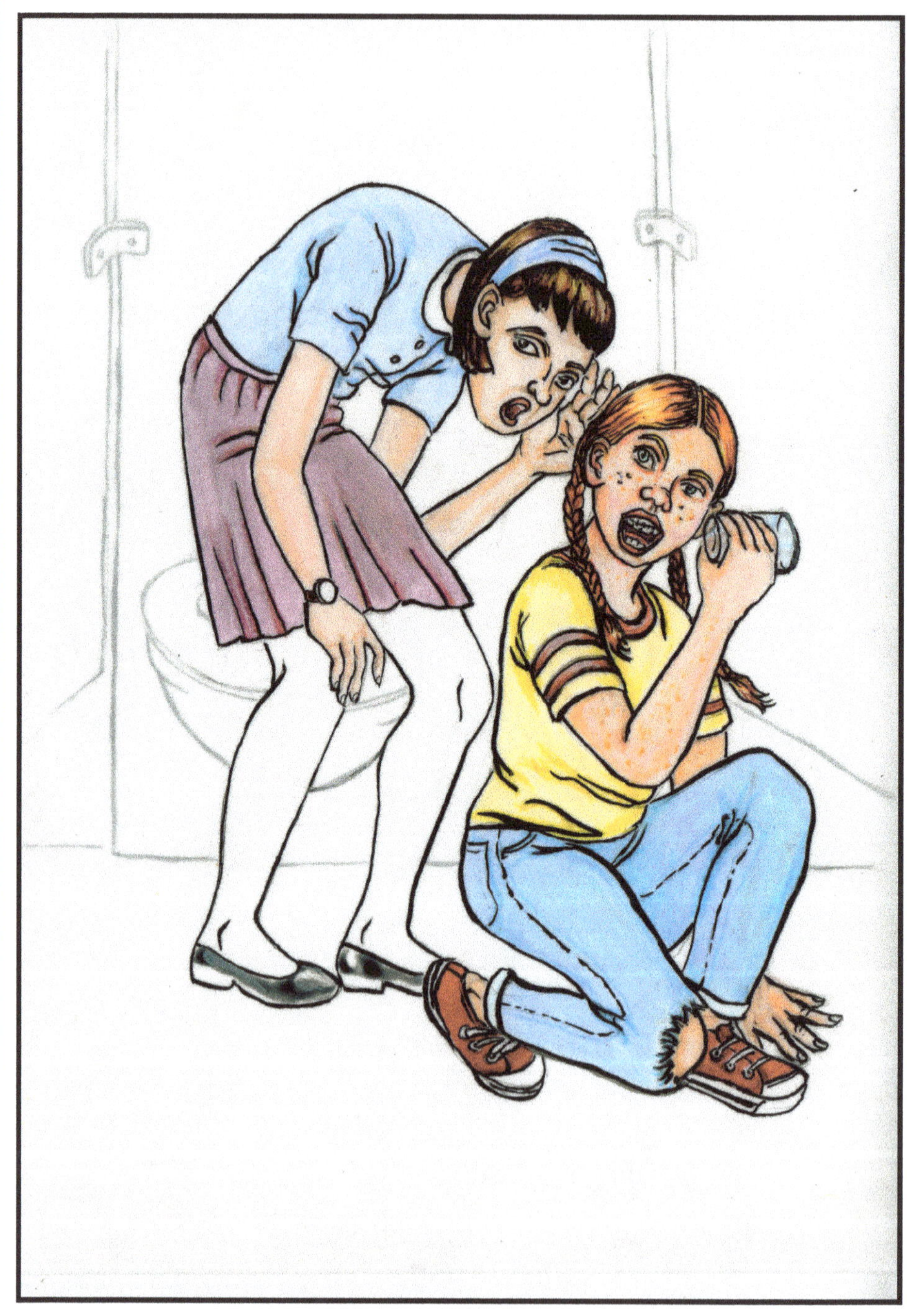

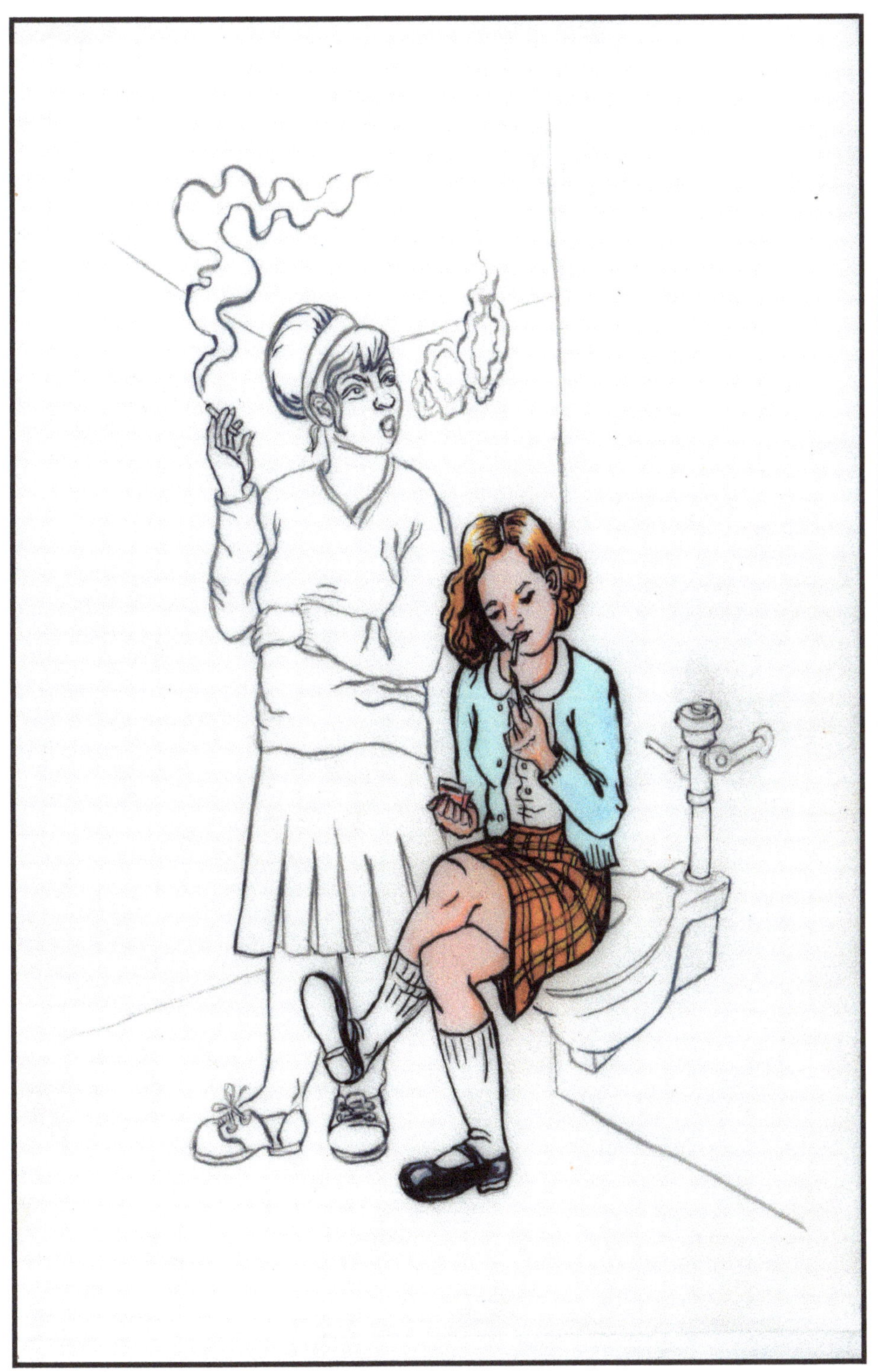

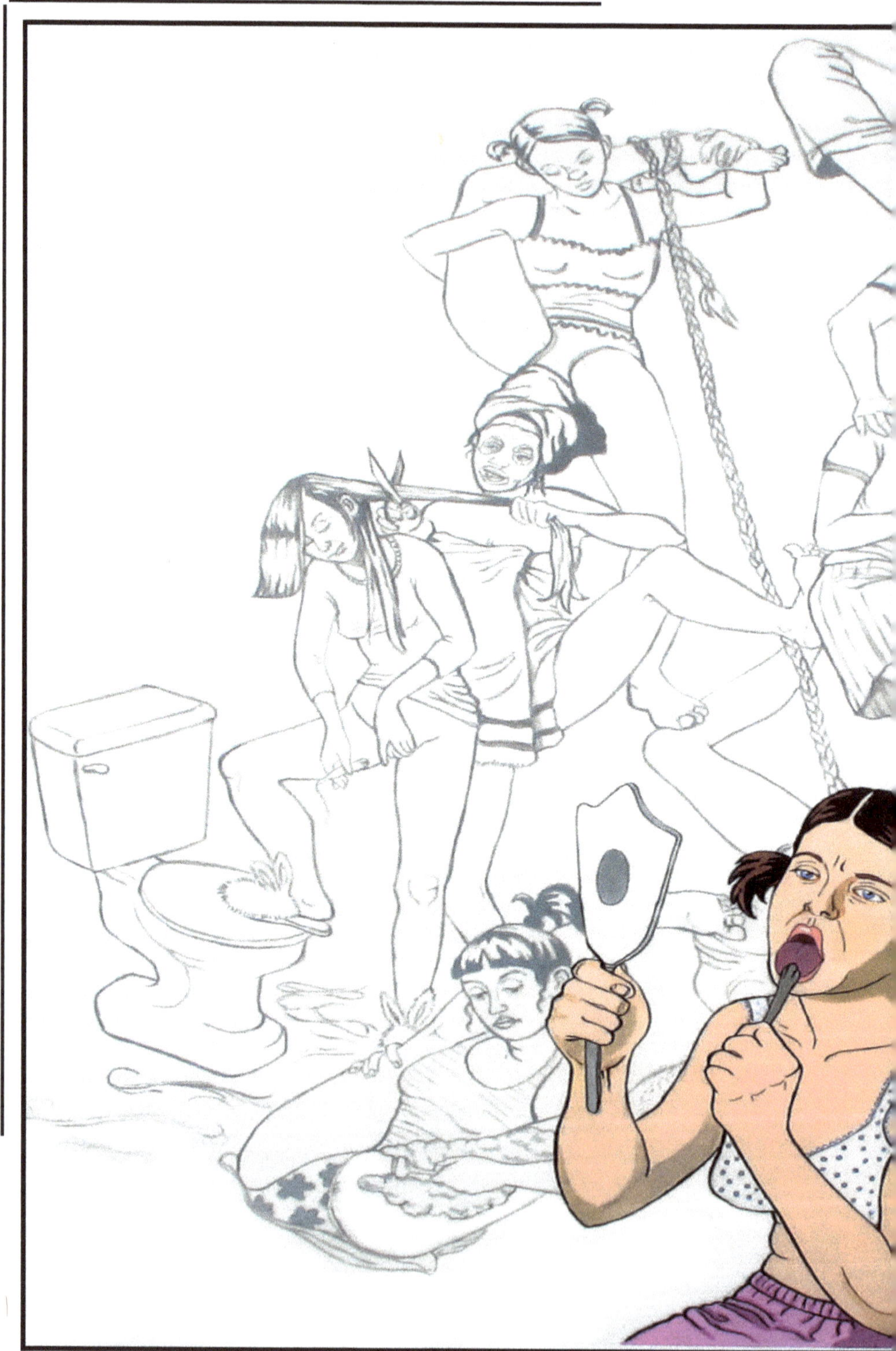

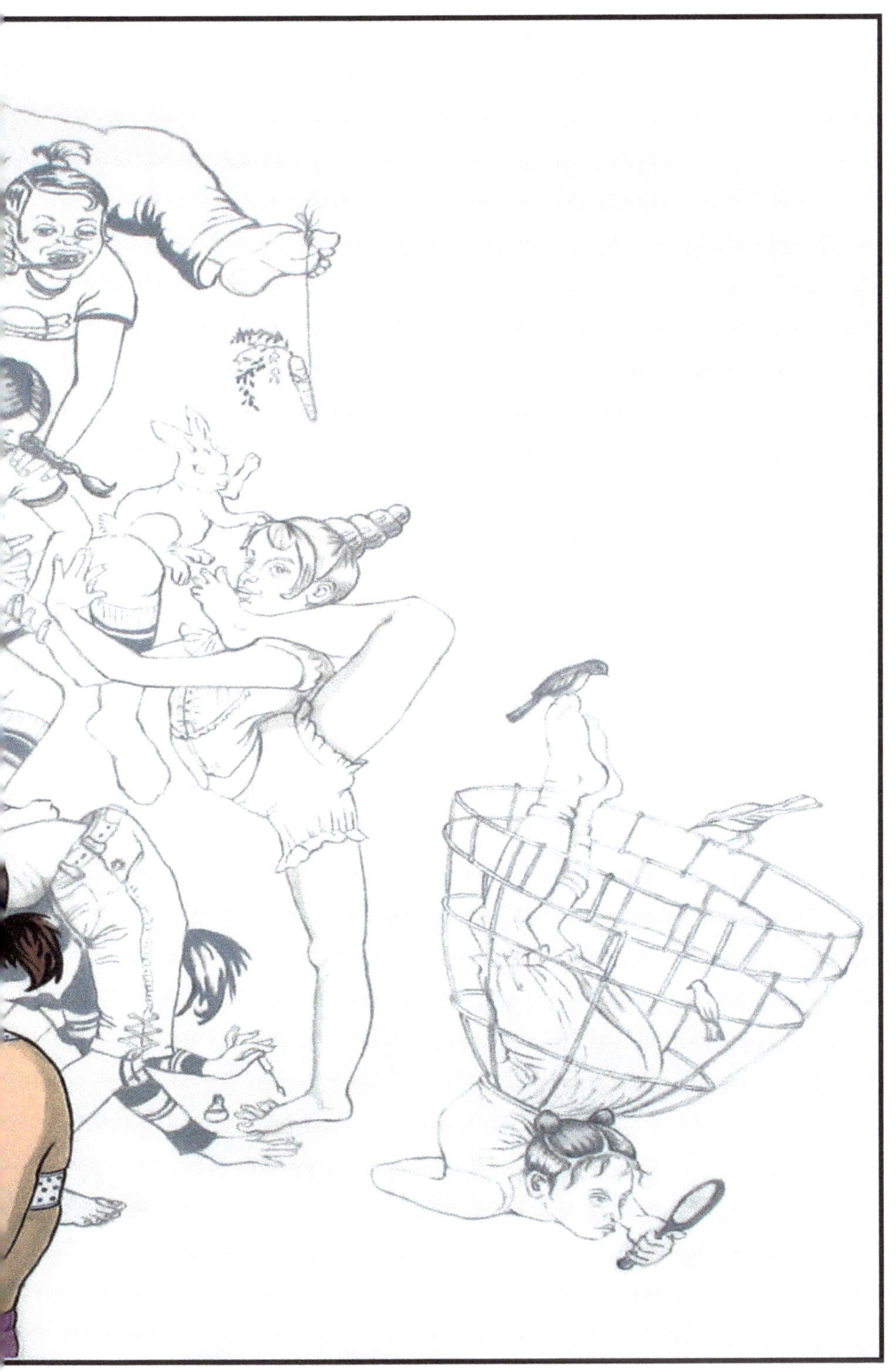

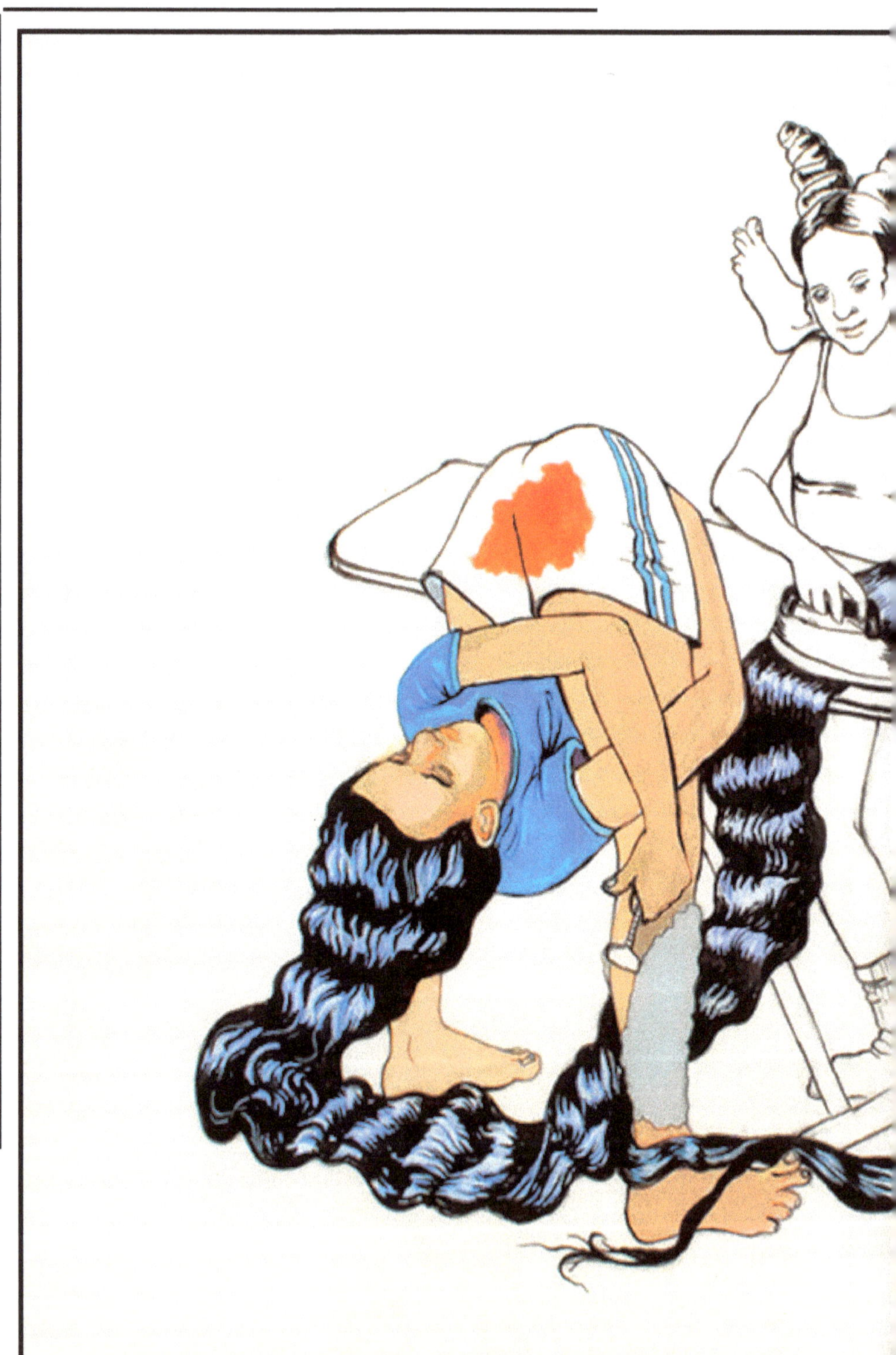

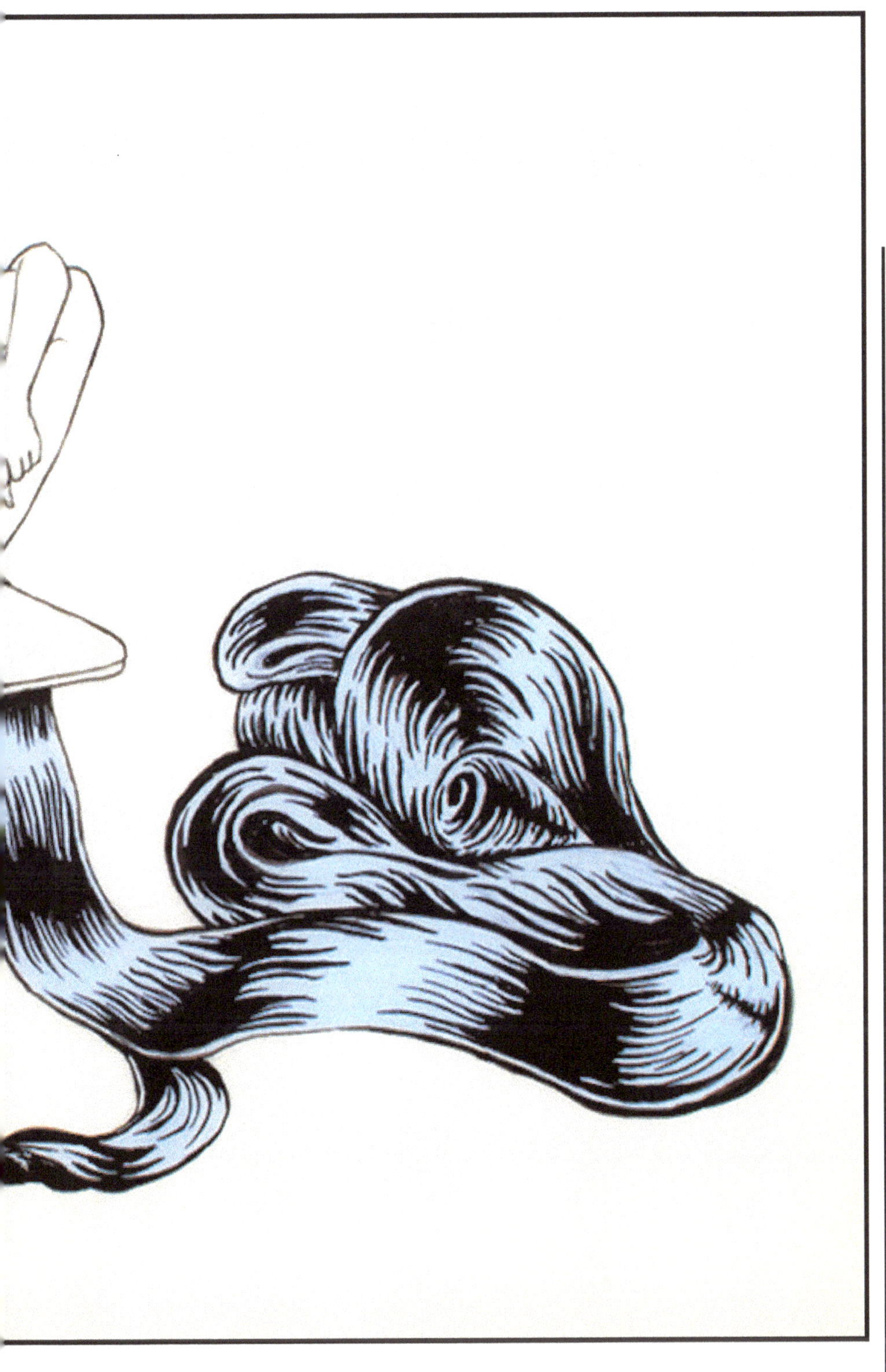

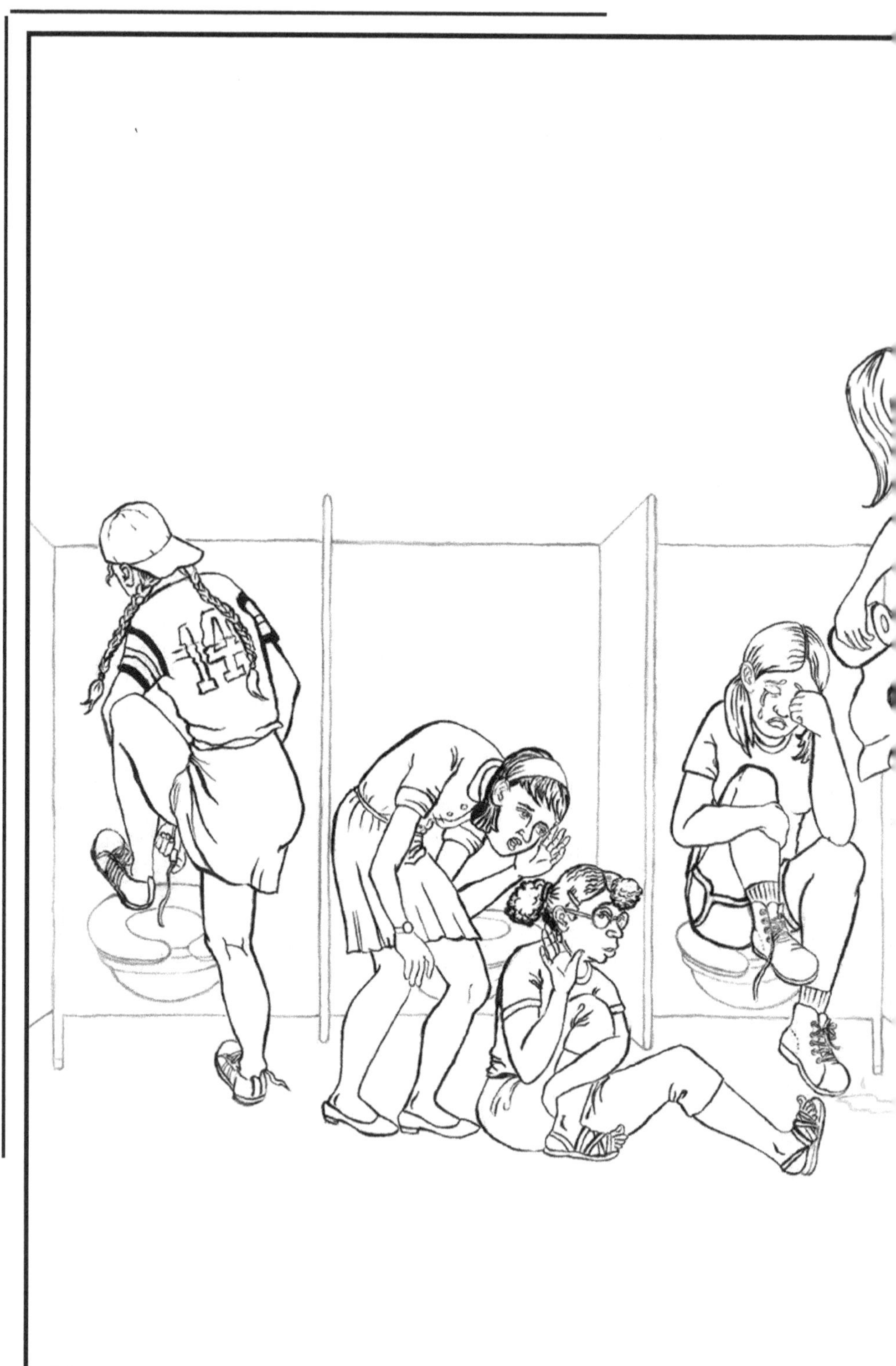

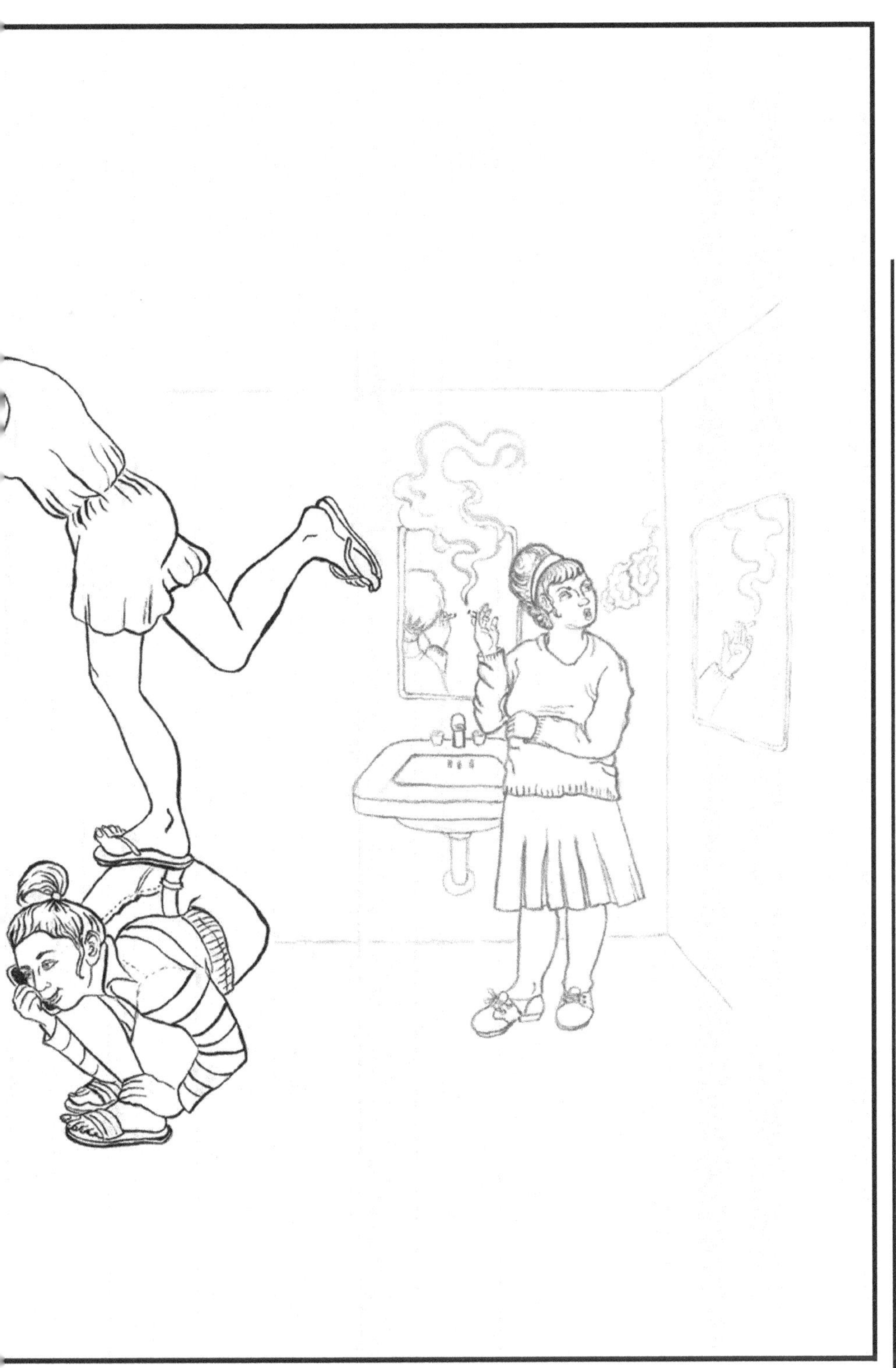

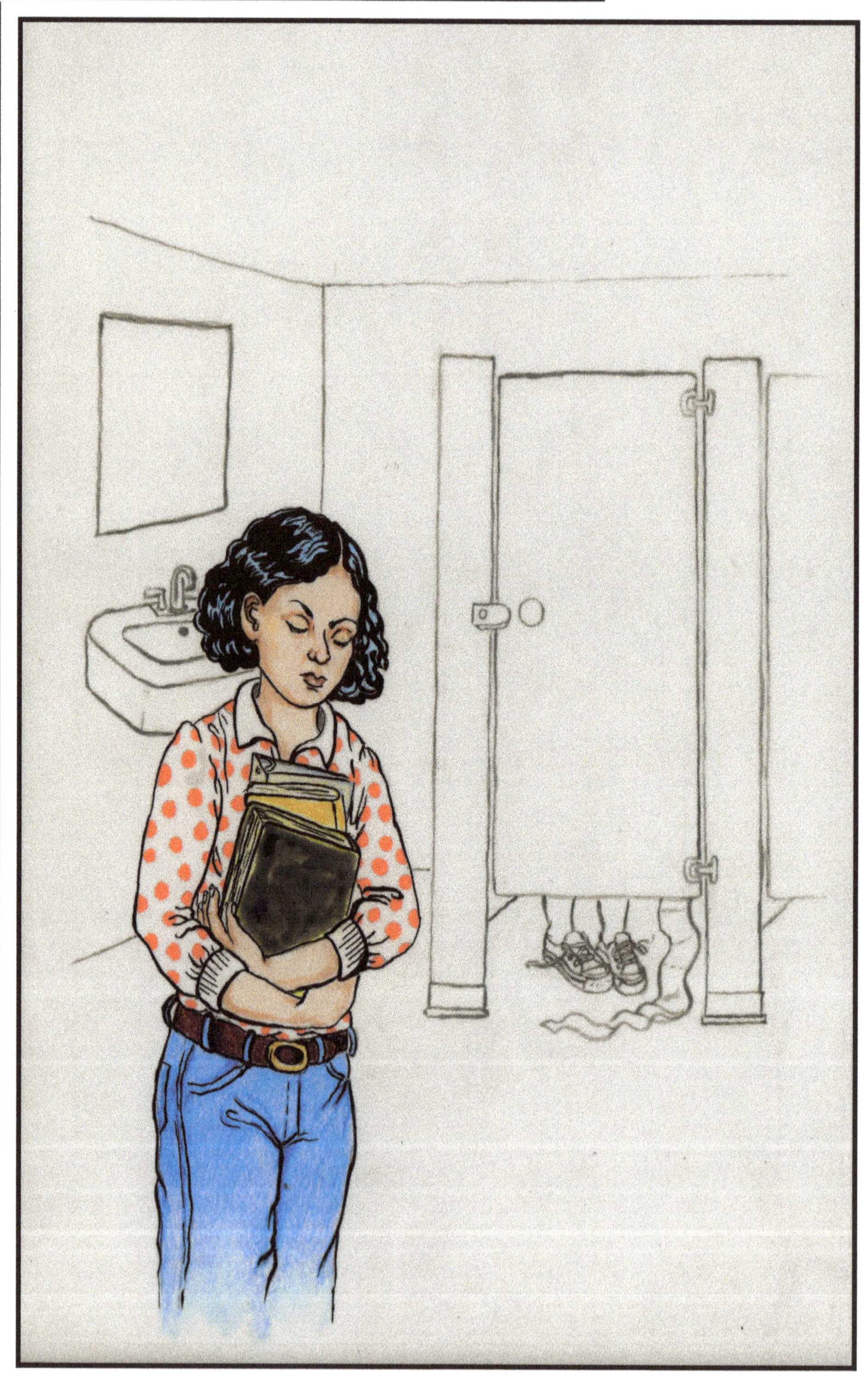

I Want to Find Love the Old-Fashioned Way: Online

Ellis Adin

Anna: I know I've always said I would *never*, but I think I'm getting desperate, Becc.

Becca: Oh my god, this is huge! I really thought you'd never come around to the idea.

Anna: I'm trying—*really trying*—to be open-minded about the whole thing. But if I'm being honest, there's still something about it that doesn't sit right with me. I just pictured something more, oh I don't know, *picturesque* for myself?

Becca: Oh, c'mon. It's not *that* bad.

Anna: (*Scoffs*) That bad? To even imagine...that *that's* our story. For the rest of my life, I'd feel compelled to create charming, beautiful little lies about how he dazzled me on Tinder, swept me off my feet on Bumble. How I absolutely fell for the bare amount of information provided to me: his age, employment at J.P. Morgan, and one-liner about that exquisite Uber rating of his. Anything but the truth. I mean, what would I tell our grandchildren!? Just the thought is horrifying—the *slime* of revealing that we really met....(*whispers*) in-person.

Becca: Face it, Anna: finding good, old-fashioned love online just isn't what it used to be. Swiping seems golden and all, it really does, but it's time to lay that baby to rest. I know some great couples that met in-person, you'd never even guess! Who *cares* if you end up locking eyes in the check-out line of Whole Foods? Sometimes people click in mysterious ways!

Anna: My mother would cringe. God, I was born in the wrong decade.

Becca: Times are changing, Ann! Just accept that people don't meet the way our parents used to.

Anna: *Well*, call me a rom-an-tic. Doesn't every little girl grow up dreaming about the day she'll meet The One? Even now, I want it to be just like my mom and dad: 11:08pm on a Wednesday; my father, returned home from the city, laying in his twin-sized childhood bed, using only his index finger and half his attention span, sliding into my dear mom's direct messages, saying the most incredible flatteries like "Waz goin on" and "Hm, that ur brother in the second pic?"

Becca: Those were the Roaring 20s, Ann! It was different, people really

didn't—
couldn't—get outsi—

Anna: It's not only that! It's the chivalry, the effort! Is that too much to ask for!?

Becca: Well, in my personal exper—

Anna: —and come to think of it, the whole concept of being "in-person" is wrong....the behavior it enables! The CHOICE paralysis! When you're out in the world you're *surrounded* by people! That's the problem if you ask me! The amount of options...it just *encourages* you to keep looking and looking!

Becca: (*Twiddles thumbs*)

Anna: In any case, I want something serious. Everyone knows that guys in real life are looking for one thing, and one thing only. They don't want personality, humor, connection...none of it! And if you're not a pretty face, well sorry kid, you missed your shot. It's like, aren't you even *curious* about my Top 3 Favorite TV Shows? Don't you even *care* how adventurous and suspiciously bronze I look scuba diving in the Galapagos? Can you at least *try* to make a quip at how much you too love tacos and Sunday Funday? It's like they don't even want to find love. On to the next one, honey. It's all so superficial!

Becca: (*Stares at clock*)

Anna: (*Sobbing into hands*).......it's just *really* hard to tell if he's 5'10" or 5'11" in the flesh......(*sighs*)....and now all of a sudden it's "rude" to ask?!

Becca: Dammit, Anna! You're too freakin' picky!

Anna continues: (*Wiping tears*) Easy for you to say, you're with Joe now.

Becca: Oh, dammit, Anna! You do know me and Joe met volunteering at the community garden, don't you?

Anna: Really? Oh, well, good for you, Bec. I could have sworn you said Hinge instead of hedge. You seem happy, that's good Bec. But between friends, I really think there's a better match for you out there. You do know there's an algorithm for that.

Tall Man Lettering

Jodie Childers

After wEEks of heated deliberation in our eSTEAMed capitOL, the city coun-CIL has voted against the Divinely Elected Prince's proposal tO mandate the use of capitAL letters to differentiate between homophones and commonly confused and misspelled words in all written documents.

According tO the Divinely Elected Prince's Office of Legal CounSEL, the law will go into EFFect anyway.

Some critics of the NEW legislation argue that these regulations may nega-tively AFFect the publishing industry. H. H. Schiller, the city's princiPAL word manufacturer, spoke out against the decree: "IT'S ludicrous. IT'S just another blow from this frog prince whO'S made it clear that he's bent on destroying free enterprize in this city. How are we going tO reprint the klassix and pub-lish the hottest NEW works tOO?"

A spokesperson from the DEP's office responded: "Look, I respect Schiller and all of his guys, BUT, WE'RE talking about princiPLEs hERE. ThEY'RE worried about dollars and CENTS; what WE'RE talking about is common SENSE."

The Flayed Man / and You Stop in a Stranger's Fields in 1542

Art by Jeff Scott Lane
Poetry by Elizabeth Atherton

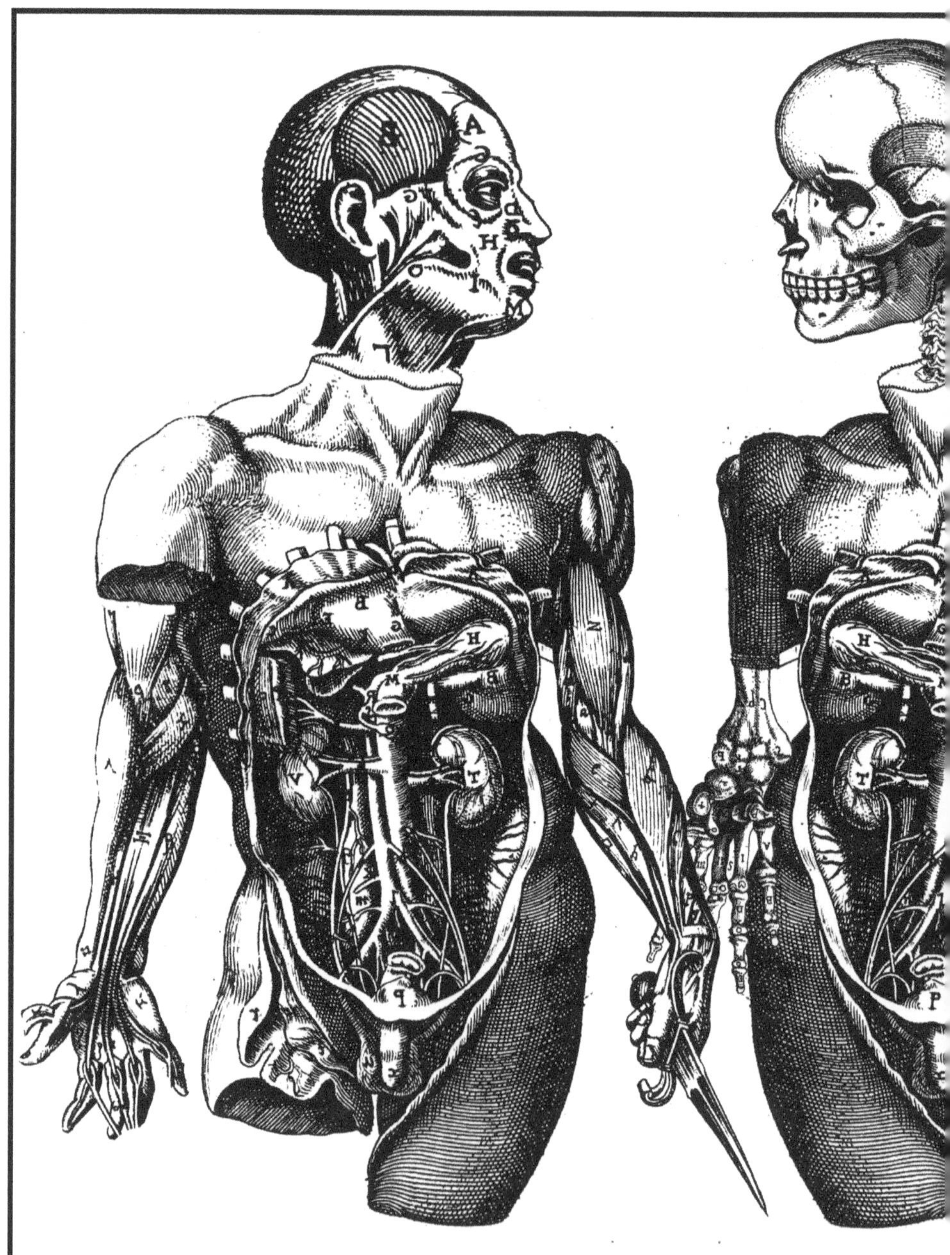

You ask for directions. You stand in the broth-colored hill, being told:
This is how you go.

The soughing in the grasses. At once
the company of the farmer is erotic. It is the eroticism
of the old friend's silhouette bumping up the path
high in the new place.

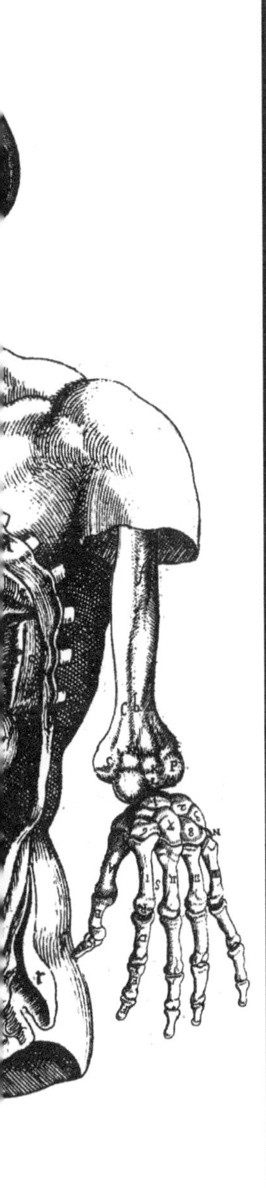

*In the diagram, the man's hand folds
on the wand of the dagger. The sporty fond lean
of the man, the operator of the human device.
Muscles marked with the letters of talk
like the little air dropped from a flute.*

Blue egg down in the nest.
Hearing from the farmer.

You see him in wonder.
He thinks you have not understood. Tenderly
he says it again, pointing.

In Order Of Appearance:

Grace Sutphin is originally from South Carolina, but currently lives in Louisville, Kentucky. Her poem Murmurations won second place in Sarabande Book's 2020 Flo Gault Poetry Prize.

Jason Hackett is a small business owner, father of four and sleep deprived. His poems can be found in The Journal of American Poetry, Slippery Elm Literary Journal, Crack the Spine, Blue River Review, Sky Island Journal, High Shelf and Cathexis Northwest Press.

Robert Oehl was born in Detroit, Michigan. After graduating from Michigan State University, he moved to New York City, eventually receiving his MFA in Photography and Printmaking from Pratt Institute. Robert has shown his work in numerous group and solo exhibitions at venues including The John Davis Gallery, Hudson, NY; The National Science and Media Museum in Bradford, UK; New Mexico History Museum, Santa Fe, New Mexico; The Holland Tunnel Gallery, Brooklyn, NY; The Visual Studies Workshop, Rochester NY; LABspace, Hillsdale, NY; Woodstock Artist Association and Museum, Woodstock, NY; and The Gallery at Marygrove College, Detroit MI. Robert is based in Hudson, New York.

Matthew Bettencourt is a student, studying Creative Writing at Madison and working as a Fiction Editor at The Madison Review.

Naomi Rhema Edwards graduated from The School of the Art Institute of Chicago with a BFA in Writing, and earned her MFA at the University of Pittsburgh. She lives in Pittsburgh.

Photographer John Sexton aims to challenge the misconception that a photo needs a pretty location to be beautiful in itself. He believes above all, a photographer needs curiosity, creativity, and a generosity of spirit to create artful pieces that tell stories that will always triumph over evanescent sunsets. He specializes in long-exposure techniques that capture notions of movement-- breaking the boundaries between photography and videography.

Skylar Rush is a writer, poet, and musician based in the swamp-filled sliver of the United States that is too far south to have a twang, and too far north to be accepted by the Caribbean. He embraces this unique Florida experience through poetry, prose, and music which focuses on the cultural medley and natural splendor of his home state.
The quirks, pitfalls, joys, and rhythms of the natural world and the human existence captivate Skylar, and he aims to provide a multi-genre reflection of the world around him. He currently studies in the Creative Writing MFA program at University of Central Florida and resides in Sanford, Florida.

Caitlin Dunn has a BFA in Creative Writing from Belhaven University. Several of her poems have been published in Belhaven's literary magazine The Brogue; her poems have won the Live Poets' Society of New Jersey poetry contest and the Southern Literary Award. She lives in Brandon, Mississippi.

Gabrielle Tribou is a graduate of Florida State University's creative writing program where she was the recipient of Florida State University's John Mackay Shaw Academy of American Poets Undergraduate Award, and a Spotlight Award in Undergraduate Fiction, selected by Pam Houston. She lives in Atlanta, Georgia, where she works as a high school English teacher.

George L Stein is a writer and photographer in the New Jersey/New York metropolitan area. Interest in monochrome, film and digital photography and urban decay/architectural subject matter has come to include street photography, fashion, fetish, collage, and oppositiional/juxtapositional projects in digital format. His work has been published in Midwest Gothic, NUNUM, Montana Mouthful, Out/Cast, The Fredericksburg Literary and Art Review, and DarkSide magazine.

Austin Newton resides in Portland, Oregon and attends Portland State University where he is a student of the BFA program for creative writing. Outside of writing, he likes to skateboard and hike. His work has previously appeared in Pathos, Portland State's literary magazine.

Bill Schulz lives in Portland, Maine. He is a writer, poet, and artist. His poetry and artwork have appeared in many periodicals over the past 40 years, including The Aurorean, The Seneca Review, Nine Mile, Nixes Mate, and The Esthetic Apostle.

Hatcher Grey is a senior in college studying fiction. He likes vintage stores, big windows and his favorite Joni Mitchell album is Court and Spark. Hatch hopes to write novels and own a dog sometime in the future.

Connor Thorpe lives in Vancouver, Canada. His work has appeared in the Antigonish Review (#177 and #189).

Charles Kell is the author of Cage of Lit Glass, chosen by Kimiko Hahn for the 2018 Autumn House Press Poetry Prize. His poetry and fiction have appeared in the New Orleans Review, The Saint Ann's Review, Kestrel, Columbia Journal, The Pinch, and elsewhere. He is Assistant Professor of English at the Community College of Rhode Island and associate editor of The Ocean State Review. He recently completed a PhD at the University of Rhode Island with a dissertation on experimental writing, criminality and transgression in the work of James Baldwin, Rosmarie Waldrop, Joanna Scott and C.D. Wright.

Divyasri Krishnan is a sixteen-year-old poet who has been writing since she could properly hold a pen. Currently, she has self-published a small poetry book called "paper crowns and paper queens" and has been the recipient of two Regional Gold Key awards through the Scholastic Art and Writing Awards. Her writing inspirations span centuries, including T.S Eliot, Philip Pullman, and the modern boykeats. When she is not writing or thinking about writing, she is breaking her back over standardized testing or running. Her thoughts and ramblings can be found @spilledhoney on Instagram.

Through the new surrealist genre Lazarus Nazario tells a story of global upheaval within the natural world. Juxtaposing images is an integral part of the work. She aims to catch the viewer off guard and have them rethink what it is they are seeing and why. Through paintings, drawings & mixed media she confronts individual, political, and collective disconnection. Lazarus creates socio-political art that is political and personal, graphic and poetic.
Recently she has been using a technique for oil paintings on aluminum and copper that mimic the look of Daguerreotypes and invoke nostalgia—the kind that has us walking in time with revised histories. Her recent work grew organically from efforts to remain powerful and poetic in the face of a looming dystopia.

Mark was born and raised in Monticello, NY. He earned a BA in Creative Writing from Valdosta State University (GA, 2010). Prior work has appeared in Forbidden Peak Press, Cathexis Northwest Press, WayMark: Voices of the Valley, and the CAPS 2020 Anthology. He lives in Woodridge, NY with his wife and kids, and is the inaugural Poet Laureate of Sullivan County, NY. Find him on Instagram @ markbpoet

Sara DiDonato was born in Naples, Italy, where her mother performed as a contortionist in a small traveling family circus. Sara received a BFA in Painting from the University of Iowa, and an MFA in Painting from the State University of New York at Albany. Her drawings and paintings have been exhibited in numerous solo and group exhibitions in national and regional venues, including the AAF Contemporary Art Fair (New York, NY); Center for the Arts Gallery, University at Buffalo; Rourke Art Museum (Morehead, MN); Albany Institute of History and Art (Albany, NY); and A.I.R. Gallery (Brooklyn, NY). Her work has been reproduced in New American Paintings and in the Stone Canoe journal. She is an Associate Professor at the State University of New York College at Brockport, where she teaches painting and drawing. She lives in Clarkson, NY with her partner, son, and three chickens.

Ellis Adin is a writer based in New York City. By day, she does business things for business people. She lives with her Chia Pet on the Upper West Side. You can follow her on Medium and Twitter @ voilaitsellis.

A New York based writer and documentary filmmaker, Jodie Childers has published essays on 20th century American political dissent, literature, music, and self-taught art. Her creative work has been published in the Portland Review, Eleven Eleven, Feral Feminisms and most recently the volume Appalachian Reckoning. Her video work has been featured in The Woody Guthrie Annual and In These Times, and she is currently directing a documentary film about Pete Seeger's environmental legacy.

Jeff Scott Lane has a BFA in the study of Graphic Design from for Virginia Commonwealth University. He has mostly worked in bookstores but spends his free time still dedicated to his art be in in the form of writing, photography, music, block printing, video, or what ever medium best suits the project. Portfolio: www.VoicesDrownedByHelvetica.com

Elizabeth Atherton is a writer and artist living in Los Angeles. Her poetry has appeared in American Chordata, Berkeley Poetry Review and Salt Hill Journal amongst other journals.

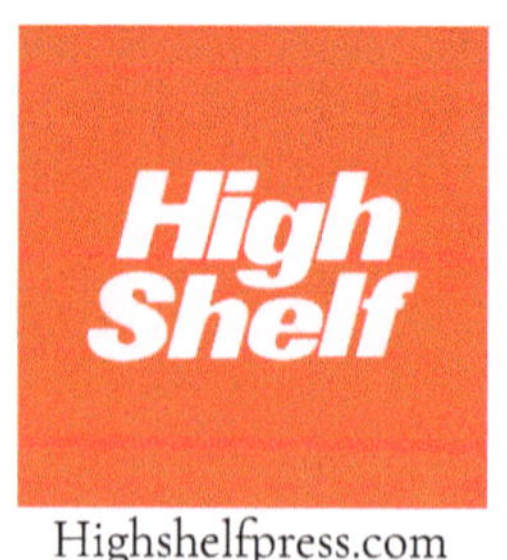

Highshelfpress.com